THEY TOO MADE AMERICA GREAT

OTHER BOOKS BY ADOLPH CASO

America's Italian Founding Fathers
* $10.00 *

Alfieri's Ode to America's Independence
* $5.00 *

Issues in Foreign Language and Bilingual Education
* $7.50 *

The Straw Obelisk (A Novel)
* $6.95 *

Water and Life (Poetry)
* $5.00 *

WORKS OF ADDITIONAL INTEREST

Italian Conversation:
A Practical Guide for Students and Travelers
By Adele Gorjanc
* $7.50 *

Early Italian Panel Painting
By Miklos Boskovitz
* $10.00 *

THEY TOO
MADE AMERICA GREAT

By
ADOLPH CASO

Boston
BRANDEN PRESS
Publishers

They Too Made America Great is available at better bookstores every-
where, or may be ordered direct from the publisher: BRANDEN PRESS *
221 Columbus Avenue * Boston, Massachusetts 02116.

To my good friends:
Josephine Tanner
Pietrina Maravigna
Giovanni Castano

CONTENTS

ILLUSTRATIONS

THEY TOO MADE AMERICA GREAT

INTRODUCTION

There is a widespread belief among Americans that the denigration of a part does not harm the whole. Italian-Americans in particular have been the butt of this misconception: the whole group has suffered for the shady reputation of a few. The intention of this book, which contains fifty short biographies of men and women of Italian descent who have contributed to America's greatness, is to help rectify this tragic mistake. The American land has given us all the potential to perfect ourselves, of which we have not taken full advantage. The greatness of the men and women whose lives are summarized here should pervade our very spirits, and make all of us better people.

From Columbus to Petrone, from Vigo to Giannini, from Paca to Sirica, from Caruso to Sinatra, the Italian-American has contributed in the most significant ways to the development and enhancement of American culture. Yet as a whole, this group has suffered the most unmerited brutalities and prejudices at the hands of fellow Americans. From the lynchings in Louisiana to the senseless mafia-craze perpetrated by the media, the Italian-American is singled out more frequently and stereotypically than any other individual.

Rodino and Sirica have helped to salvage the American democracy. Yet Senator Mondale, speaking against the Watergate scandal during his campaign for the Vice Presidency, singled out Segretti among all those who abused the principles of our Constitution.

Other examples are rife: A high-school principal in Rhode Island allowed his students to have a "mafia day" so they could have some fun. New York policemen dressed a la mafia to capture mafiosi, yet to their chagrin, they discovered hardly one Italian-American. Reporting the disappearance of James Hoffa, news commentators ascribed mafia connections only to those characters having Italian names. And in his book on the Bicentennial, Alistair Cook speaks of Al Capone, but not of Beccaria, whose humane principles have

13

been incorporated into the very documents that made and will continue to make possible the celebration of American independence.

Batman and Robin work in Gotham City in much the same manner as those who work in the United States justice department—forever pursuing mythological criminals, all the while allowing the real ones to go as they please. Valachi, Segretti, Costello—who are they in comparison to such Americans as Vigo, Mazzei, Bellanca?

Were all Italian-Americans mafiosi in the tradition of ancient Sicily, then with the abuses running rampant in America, there should be a lot more broken noses. In one sense, however, it may be true that the contemporary Italian-American does not have the *coglioni* of his forefathers: otherwise, America would not have the serial-type "prosecutions."

America, we might all remember, is a beautiful Italian name.

GIOVANNI CABOT (1435-1498): *Born in Genova; Died in Labrador*

"John" Cabot, the first European to set foot on North American soil, can rightly be considered the true discoverer of that continent. In 1497 he embarked upon a sailing expedition in behalf of Henry VII of England, and was finally to plant the British flag (as well as that of his own adopted country, the Republic of Venice) in the soil of what is now, Labrador, Canada.

Of the many Italian navigators and explorers to work for foreign countries, John Cabot was one of the few to have received some recognition (others were Sebastian Cabot, and to a certain extent, Americo Vespucci). King Henry VII referred to Cabot as his "beloved John"—a term of endearment well deserved, for had it not been for this *Genovese*, the exploration, colonization, and subsequent development of almost the entire continent of North America may have taken an entirely different course.

It is certain that the Cabot family of today, and the Lodges as well, are descended from none other than John Cabot of Genoa, and his son, Sebastian, of Venice. Regardless of claims and disclaims with respect to descendency, however, one cannot deny that this Italian devoted his life and services to benefit the people of another nation. Considering the bounties made available by the American land, Cabot's descendants can be proud to claim an Italian for their ancestor.

Sebastian Cabot can also be thanked for the role he played in England's behalf. According to Campbell, the English historian, Sebastian made England the world's leading naval power. Italian-Americans can look to the name Cabot as a symbol of the Italians' input in behalf of the progress of the western world.

Another outstanding contributor to England's history, incidentally, was also of Italian descent. Benjamin Disraeli, the great author and statesman who guided Victorian England to the peak of her power, had Jewish ancestors from the city of Cento, Italy.

John Cabot departing from England.

Sebastian Cabot (by unknown artist).

CHRISTOPHER COLUMBUS (1451-1506): *Born in Genova, Italy; Died in Spain*

In the eyes of Christopher Columbus, Arthur Ochs Sulzberger may not be too different from Bobadilla; in the eyes of many Italian-Americans, *The New York Times* is not much different from the inquisitorial royal court of fifteenth century Spain.

Regardless of who may or may not have come before him, Columbus is the discoverer of the American continents.

For his awesome undertaking of August 1492, he and he alone should be recognized as the Universal Admiral.

History has recorded many heroes: Carlton Fisk, hitting the timely homerun to keep the World Series alive; Casanova, perhaps, making love successfully to "prohibited" women; Marco Polo, meandering his way into a million truths theretofore unknown to a world that "knew" truths; Neil A. Armstrong, setting foot on the Moon, 10:56 P.M., 20 July 1969; even Leif Ericson and Vasco da Gama. Hundreds of similar heroes continue to enjoy acceptance and fame. For the Universal Admiral, such has not been the case.

Bobadilla's chains, which bolted Columbus' body to the wood of the ship, remain as strong to this very day.

Yet, does the world know of a greater hero? Is there another individual whose origin has been claimed by so many nations? Did not Hitler command his scholars to prove that Christoph was German? Did not Portuguese youngsters know Colon's ancestors?

Although Puerto Ricans and Latin American students know that Cristobal was a Spaniard, editors of certain encyclopedias are not sure:

"We think that Columbus was born in Genoa, Italy . . . (but) probably had never heard of the Scandinavians like Leif Ericson, who had explored North America in the 10th century. Columbus is said to have visited Iceland in 1477, and he may have talked there (for he knew Latin) to the people who knew about those early voyagers."

"But the fact remains, boys and girls," says Mickey Mouse

18

Christopher Columbus (by unknown artist).

in Disney's *Wonderful World of Knowledge*, "that the Vikings discovered America 500 years before Columbus.

In many American public schools, built during the early part of the twentieth century, at a time when Nietzcheism was running its course, it is not difficult to find depicted blond-blue-eyed Vikings lead ashore by Leif Ericson, thus beginning the colonization of the American land. That Leif Ericson may have found his way down the coast of New England, even to settle Waltham, is possible; that he told the world the whereabouts of Boston just did not happen.

History has played an awful trick on these two men. They've been brought together to the exclusion of one another. Yet, each followed his own life style, without any physical or historical connection between them. One cannot speak well of Leif Ericson and of Christopher Columbus at the same time. When in 1965, for instance, the world spoke of Ericson, it spoke of him in laudatory terms; at the same time, it made Columbus a scapegoat if not a fraud. Honor vs. dishonor, and the year 1965 marks the biggest blow to Columbus' reputation.

In the introductory chapter of *Age of Exploration*, published by Time-Life, J. R. Hale reproduces the newly discovered map of the "New World", clearly showing Vinland and part of North America. It had been drawn by a Swiss Monk in about 1440, based on information furnished by the Vikings, and uncovered by a group of famous Yale University and British Museum scholars. The discovery, as one can imagine, was so significant that George Painter exuberantly claimed it "the most tremendous historical discovery of the twentieth century."

The *American Heritage* magazine (October, 1965) reproduced the same map, enlarged to cover two full pages. *Newsweek, Time, The New York Times*, and other leading magazines and newspapers carried lengthy front page articles with ample space given to the map.

"The map throws further doubt on the legend that Columbus was sailing into completely mysterious and uncharted seas when he set out with his small fleet in 1492. Instead,

20

it appears possible that the Viking voyages may have served as an incentive to Columbus and Cabot and other rediscoverers of America in the 15th century," reported the distinguished editors of *Time* magazine.

Printing first-page articles with map, *The New York Times* further made hay with a rebuttal of Italian-Americans who, without a doubt, must have marched in the Columbus Day parade with who knows what dampened spirits. The disclosure, after all, had been made the day before the parade.

The gloating that took place in the United States was to be expected. Had not those Italian-Americans made so much fuss over the fact that an Italian had made America possible, and all of that?

And, had not Angelo Noce—not Ted Smith, John Taylor, Mr. Jones or Sulzberger—lobbied in the state of Colorado to establish "Columbus Day," which was then "imposed on the rest of the nation?"

Now that the Vinland map had finally been discovered, the critics of Columbus needed no longer be skeptical of the Viking voyages. Even Fiorello La Guardia, had he been alive, might have gloated over the event. When he was Mayor and erected a statue to Ericson, many Italian-Americans criticized him for the great fanfare and deep-felt eulogies over the historical feats of the Vikings. It is said that Fiorello even relegated a statue of Romulus and Remus suckling the She Wolf into a corner of a basement. With the exception, perhaps, of the noise made by some vociferous and unwitty Italian-Americans, there was not any fanfare over any statue erected on behalf of Columbus.

In April, 1966—not October 11, 1966—news broke that the Vinland map was a forgery.

A simple test of the ink showed that it had been drawn in the nineteenth century.

Those leading editors, who had had a field day with the discovery of that map, now either completely disregarded the forgery or made brief allusions with such titles as "The Map Flap"—and did little, if anything else. Columbus, of course, was never vindicated.

21

George Painter, Lawrence Witten, Alexander Vietor, and Thomas Marston, who had made the historical announcements on the eve of America's Columbus Day celebration, have not come forth with an apology.

One should not be surprised if these great scholars have not been rewarded with promotions to full professorships, both for their "eight years" of research on the forged Vinland map and for their machinations over the timely announcement of their unprecedented scholarly research results. With their newly acquired research skills and expertise, they could be asked to look into the matter of Johann Fust and the invention of the printing press, or even "caveat" over Antonio Meucci, the inventor of the telephone. Considering the harm they've done, however, it might be better were they to go pack sand instead.

When encyclopedists say, "We think that Columbus was born in Genoa," they cast doubt on a fact which, after four centuries of research, still remains the same.

When editors speak of "the legend that Columbus was sailing into completely mysterious and uncharted seas," with the word "legend" they consciously attempt to destroy the accomplishments of the man. That he made four voyages to the New World without making one single navigational error in either direction is an achievement greater than landing man on the moon, if one considers the communication networks now available and in support from every corner of the earth.

Yet, Columbus, assisted by a crew of less than one hundred men, many of whom had been criminals in Spanish jails, hit the "bull's eye" some three thousand miles away, all on his own.

He charted the uncharted waters, all on his own. He guided, cajoled, and controlled his crew, all on his own. He made sailors out of criminals, all on his own. He showed the courageous Spaniards—those who decided to brave the ocean only after its waters had been scientifically charted, how to make an egg stand on one end, all on his own.

These facts have been proved. They can never be used

as basis for legends; indeed, they destroy them because legends grow out of man's imagination which make them seem real through the clever, if not unconscious use of verisimilitudes. If any, the Vikings are the perfect matter for legends. So much of what they did or did not do was always enveloped in the perennial northern clouds that often hide reality, let alone truth itself.

Had they discovered anything, they would have told the world. Just as Marco Polo did. Just as Columbus told the world that he had found the route to the East by sailing West, and assuring everyone, but especially the Spaniards, that beyond the pillars of Hercules there were no monsters or precipitous falls. Just as Vespucci told the world that Columbus had discovered the New World.

Considering the vantage point the Vikings had, and one should easily see the degree of daring, the difference of challenge in the tenth-century Vikings and the fifteenth-century men of the Renaissance.

The trek of the Vikings was as follows: about 250 miles from the Shetland to Faeroe Island; about 300 miles from Faeroe to Greenland; about 250 miles from Greenland to Newfoundland; and about 500 miles of coasts from Newfoundland to Boston.

At no time did Leif Ericson or his ancestors sail much more than 300 miles of open waters.

Columbus, on the other hand, sailed about 3,000 miles of open and uncharted waters, following a route that would have taken him directly into the Panamanian coast, with the Pacific on the other side, had he not run into Cuba and Puerto Rico. And it must not be forgotten that he was the first to reach the coast of Panama during his last voyage of 1502.

There is a map that Columbus consulted, however. It was the one published by Paolo dal Pozzo Toscanelli in 1474. Toscanelli was a Florentine scientist convinced of the earth's sphericity. He knew that the Orient could be reached by going westward. As a result, Toscanelli drew a map of a circular world with several bodies of land scattered between

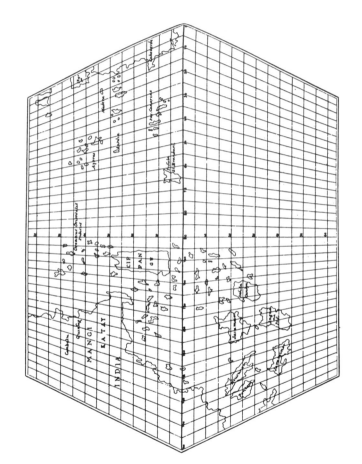

Toscanelli's map of 1474 (from *Attraverso I Secoli*).

Katay and the Canary Islands which had been discovered in 1270 by an Italian named Malocello. Toscanelli's map was widely known in Europe; yet neither the American magazine editors, or those of the *Age of Exploration*, or those of *The New York Times*, mention this rather well known fact. Following the voyages of Columbus and of Vespucci, another map was made based on the information furnished by them and published in 1052; it was the map of another Italian named Caveri.

That Columbus was a born sailor is well-known. In 1474, hardly twenty-three years old, he was rendering service on ships belonging to his native city of Genova. On a voyage toward England in 1476, pirates attacked the ship, causing the young Columbus to take refuge in Portugal, where he subsequently approached King John II to discuss his plan on how to reach the Orient. The King, however, summarily dismissed him.

He went to Spain where he succeeded in gaining an audience with King Ferdinand and his wife, Queen Isabella. They listened, but turned the plan to the experts of the royal court. Upon examining it, they concluded that Columbus was a lunatic and that the plan was as absurd as the ideas behind it. The Spanish king, therefore, rejected it.

Discouraged by the reception of the Spaniards, but unaware of Queen Isabella's favorable intuition, Columbus set out for France, in hopes of being received by the French court. Before he could reach the boundaries, he was approached by a group of royal soldiers on horseback with orders to have him return to Isabella. As a result, three ships were made available: the *Nina*, the *Pinto*, and the *Santa Maria*.

Though the rest is history, what should be added is something very few historians talk about: The *Santa Maria* was leased by Columbus himself. The *Nina* and the *Pinta*, on the other hand, were furnished by the city of Palos, "in payment of a fine owed to the Queen." Considering the crew and where it was gotten, and the ships and how they were gotten, any one should see that it was Columbus who made the largest capital outlay. Considering what Columbus got in return, and comparing it to what Spain got in return, and the argument becomes untenable.

He departed from the port of Palos on August 3, 1492. He was forty-one years old.

On October 12, 1492, after a journey filled with all kinds of personnel problems, including mutiny, he reached San Salvador in the Bahamas, not knowing he had struck new land. Its people he called Indians, thinking he had landed on some part of India.

In his subsequent three voyages of 1493, 1498, and 1502, he searched to locate the whereabouts of the true Orientals and the passage to the East. The Spaniards, meanwhile, searched for gold.

Bobadilla, the Spanish emissary, put an end to Columbus' wanderings. He shackled the irascible Admiral and returned him to Spain in chains. Had Columbus found gold, his fate surely would have been different.

"We Spaniards suffer from a disease that only gold can cure," admitted Hernando Cortes some years later.

Envy would have destroyed Columbus even if he had found gold; futile was his attempt to be recognized by his fellow men for the feats he had accomplished—feats that go beyond the discovery of territories, although as a result, American gold enriched Spain to the point that it became the super power of the world, thanks to another Italian, Giulio Alberoni, who was its distinguished prime minister at this time.

Columbus' accomplishments went beyond his leadership abilities, his navagational skills, and his prowess as a discoverer and explorer. His contributions to science are of enormous importance. He contributed toward the discovery of the declination of the magnetic needle, and toward the discovery of the line without the magnetic declination. He discovered the laws of the rotation of the winds, the reliefs of the equatorial and Gulf Stream currents, the effects of humidity and rain, and several other items dealing with nautical astronomy.

Many years after his un-noticed death, after the world

learned of what the Universal Admiral had really accomplished, many sought to preserve his bones, first buried in Seville. They were subsequently transported to Haiti and then to Cuba, and back to Seville, whatever was left of them. It should be added that the United States could have claimed those bones after the War of 1898 when it defeated Spain. But if the United States did not claim Columbus' bones, neither did Italy.

With the passing of time, and in spite of all the disclaims against him, Columbus has grown in stature. King's College is now Columbia University. There is the song, "Columbia, the gem of the Ocean." Yet the man continues to be the object of cynical and damaging criticism. He has become fair game, perhaps because he himself is the point of reference the likes of no man: everything has to be judged by and through him. Yet, it is difficult to understand the vicious attacks on Columbus by *The New York Times*. That Columbus was an Italian may explain the attacks.

He was an Italian, and the Italian-Americans love him. When the Vinland map was made public and the paper carried in the manner it did, with comments that were duly derogatory, the Italian-Americans protested. The editors of the newspaper, however, accused them of conducting a "scholarly vendetta" against Yale University.

Reading the title of the article, "Columbus's Crew Won't Switch" which carries a stigma if not the insinuation that has been typical of this newspaper, one should see who is practicing a vendetta.

Philip Benjamin, the author of the article, knew all too well that the real "crew" of Columbus was made up of many criminals. It does not take much intelligence, therefore, to see the dishonor that this paper insists on inflicting on an entire segment of U.S. citizens—those of Italian backgrounds who have given more than just their sweat and blood in behalf of America.

"Bad News for Columbus, Perhaps" is the title of another article prominently printed in *The New York Times*. It tells about new discoveries that prove that Africans arrived

Christopher Columbus (by an unknown artist).

Christopher Columbus (by unknown artist).

in America prior to Columbus. As strange as it may be however, Ivan Van Sertina did not say that Columbus had traveled to Brazzaville deep in the Congo to learn about the secret passage to the East by sailing west.

The issue is not Columbus, but the manner that *The New York Times* editors have been denigrating some twenty-five or more millions of American citizens of Italian heritage. They forget that the Italians revealed the American continents to the world, and that they also made possible the foundations of the U.S. form of government, from its Declaration of Causes, written only in English and in Italian, to that of Independence, together with the Constitution and the Bill of Rights—all based on Italian ideas and thoughts.

Editors in general, and those of *The New York Times* specifically, have chosen to remain silent regarding these contributions. They should be remorseful over the fact that they prefer to denigrate a whole group of people rather than appreciate their role in making, in shaping, and in maintaining this great and democratic nation. Their editorials often speak on the dignity of man. All the while, they brutalize mankind.

AMERICO VESPUCCI (1454-1512): *Born in Florence; Died in Seville*

Americo Vespucci was perhaps the luckiest of the Italian navigators of his time. That he died a natural death—and in Spain, of all places—was good fortune enough. That the continents of North and South America bear his name (rather than that of Christopher Columbus) is for Vespucci, lucky indeed.

In one sense, Vespucci's claim as discoverer of the New World is entirely correct: it was he who recognized that the land mass that Columbus', the Cabots', and his own ships had reached was neither China nor India, but an entirely new world. Vespucci brought this information back to Europe, and proceeded to promulgate it. As a result, the German cartographer, Martin Waldeseemuller published a map of the New World, on which was printed the name "America." That Waldeseemuller failed to give Columbus due credit is understandable (though not acceptable) in light of the disrepute and ultimate oblivion into which Columbus' name had fallen.

Had the new world borne the name of a non-Italian, as could easily have happened, it surely would have been the greatest injustice of all. When one considers the glory, wealth, and power that has come to Spain, England, Portugal, and France through the services of the Italian explorers of the *Rinascimento*—in contrast to the minimal rewards derived by Italy, itself—one must conclude that a certain justice has been done in naming the new continent "America." Fortune, for once, was on Italy's side.

Editors of the Penguin Books claim that America was named not after the "silly and pretentious" Italian, but after Amerik, an English merchant who helped finance Cabot's voyage. Yet the editors do not point to a single document prior to Waldeseemuller's map that bears Amerik's name.

Vespucci was a great mariner. He made possible the colonization of Brazil by Portugal, and the most extensive exploration of the New World. He also contributed to the

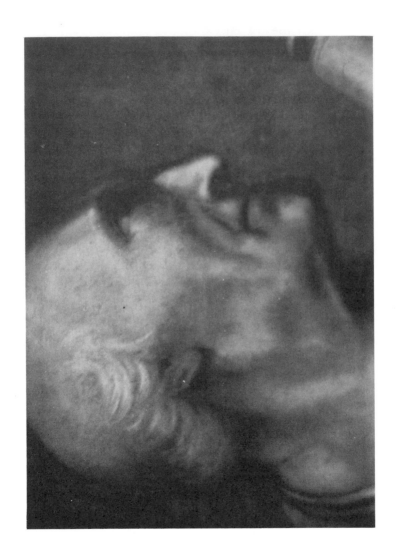

Americo Vespucci (by unknown artist).

field of navigation, making important discoveries regarding the scientific use of the longitude. In light of his contributions, we might conclude that Americo deserved whatever credit he got. He was recognized during his lifetime as Spain's "Piloto Mayor." He is also remembered by the state of Georgia: the city Americus is situated east of the great city of Columbus.

Ironically, Vespucci did for the New World what Marco Polo had done some 200 years earlier for the Orient. Whereas Vespucci's observations were believed, those of Marco Polo, though also true, were never accepted. Marco Polo's contemporaries, however, were quick to make destructive use of Chinese gunpowder, which he had brought to Europe.

GIOVANNI DA VERRAZZANO (1485-1527): *Born in Florence; Died in Spain*

Many of the Italian explorers who went to sea or ventured into uncharted lands suffered grievously at the hands of Spain. Columbus was put in chains for two months; Fathers Chino and da Nizza were abused and ridiculed; Malaspina was jailed for about six years, his scientific research scattered by the Spaniards. However, unlike Columbus, Chino, da Nizza, and Malaspina, who were at least allowed to die in oblivion, Giovanni da Verrazzano, who had discovered the Hudson and a good part of Canada for France was captured by the Spaniards and brought to Spain for an out-and-out massacre.

Verrazzano's name is now being revived, thanks to the efforts of the Italian Historical Society of New York. The Society had to fight for years to have the bridge spanning the Hudson River named for Verrazzano, the river's authentic discoverer. Yet, though people usually refer to the structure as the "Verrazzano" Bridge, its real name is the Verrazzano-Narrows Bridge. Scant recognition, indeed!

Verrazzano's misfortune, however, continues. Recently, a group of Italian Americans attempted to create an institution of higher learning, which they called the Verrazzano College. After hardly a year of classes, the college closed.

As a young man, Giovanni da Verrazzano had spent several years on the open seas. His chance for glory finally came through Francis I of France, who had wanted without success to plant the French flag on the New World. When his own admirals failed to achieve that goal, Francis turned to two Italians to fulfill his wish—Antonio Gondi to help finance the expedition, and Verrazzano to lead it.

Twelve years before Cartier was to set foot on Canadian soil, Verrazzano had already sailed along the North American coastline, and proceeded from the Carolines to the tip of Newfoundland and back to France. He believed that beyond the Carolines lay the "Verrazzano" sea (the Pacific

Giovanni da Verrazzano (National Gallery of Art).

Ocean), and was convinced that somewhere along the eastern coast of North America lay a passage to this body of water— and a better route to the China mainland.

Although he never discovered the coveted trade route, Verrazzano was the first to sail up the Hudson River. Where the present city of New York towers above what he described as a sweet "Laurel forest," Verrazzano planted the French flag. He thus made possible France's future colonization of Canada and Louisiana. Nevertheless, with the exception of a small bay named in Verrazzano's honor—a bay that even the more important atlases neglect to mention—this Florentine navigator and his accomplishments have been practically forgotten.

Bestowing honor to so great a man, the Italian Americans of New York had to fight the most unreasonable battles with their fellow Americans, who for some inexplicable reason wish to foreget the sacrifices made by Columbus, Caboto, Vespucci, and Verrazzano. Verrazzano did as much to help France become an international power as Giulio Mazzarino (Cardinal Mazarin) did some 150 years later, when he put France's finances and politics in order, allowing that country to enjoy the extravagant affluence of the court of Louis XIV.

Neither France nor Italy claimed Verrazzano's bones. And if we remember Henry Hudson—and not Verrazzano—in the name of the Hudson River and Bay, many New Yorkers do not give Verrazzano the recognition of naming even a bridge entirely in his honor.

MARCO DA NIZZA (1510-1558): *Born in Nizza; Died in Mexico*

Today the name Marcos de Niza, as it is generally spelled, is seeing somewhat of a revival, thanks to the efforts of Black American historians who have documented and publicized the career of the explorer, Esteban. Leading the way into unknown Arizona, Estaban was killed by Indians; and Friar Marco traveled through mountainous territory, reaching as far west as what is now Phoenix, Arizona. There he planted the Cross of Christ and left an inscription on a huge rock.

Although Marco did not find Cibola, he reported to his Spanish leaders that he had discovered a city "greater than the city of Mexico"; and his statement prompted Coronado to lead an expedition into Arizona. When the conquistadores of North America failed to find gold, they took our their wrath on the poor friar, cursing him for having led them on a two-year-long wild-goose chase. As a result, Friar Marco is said to have taken ill and died.

The North American Indians, who had not discovered gold as had the Incas, Mayans, and Aztecs, were not victims of the white men's lust for the yellow wealth—a lust that would have destroyed these Indians as surely as it had caused the extermination of the affluent Indian cultures in South America. All in the name of God and for the sake of gold.

The discoverer of the Sonora Valley in Nebraska, and perhaps territory of Arizona as well, Friar Marco made several interesting studies of the Indians. He was among the first to try to understand and describe their psychological make-up.

Whether or not Friar Marco deliberately lied to the Spaniards has been considered by Bandelier, who points out that desert heat has an adverse effect on human vision. It is also possible, Bandelier observes, that Marco had come across a city which he had compared "with the newly found Spanish town of Mexico, not with the old city which had been destroyed in 1521."

37

Marco da Nizza (from Giovanni Schiavo, *Four Centuries of Italian American History.)*

Regardless of what else may be said, this singular Italian, born in what is today known as the French Riviera, opened the way for the exploration and eventual settlement of the vast lands of New Mexico, Arizona, and Nebraska.

FRANCESCO CHINO (1645-1711): *Born in Segno, Italy; Died in New Mexico*

After about 230 years of almost complete obscurity, Father Francesco Eusebio Chino is now beginning to receive the credit and the respect he truly deserves. Thanks are due to H. E. Bolton, who in 1919 translated and published Chino's *Favores Celestiales.*

Father Chino (Kino in Spanish) enjoyed the kind of "recognition" the Spaniards have bestowed on Columbus, da Nizza, and Malaspina. Yet these four Italians may have done more for the Spanish-speaking world than many people will acknowledge.

Father Chino, who received his higher education from the University of Freiburg in Germany, wished to go to China as a mathematician. The Jesuits, however, decreed that he become a missionary with the Spaniards in Mexico, where he landed in 1681.

After observing the appearance and passing of the comet of 1680, Chino wrote and published, *Exposicion Astronomica de el Cometa.* When this book began to enjoy some popularity, a Jesuit colleague, Siguenza y Gongora, quickly moved to discredit Chino, publishing a scathing attack on his Italian brother. However, Father Chino went on with his mission unperturbed.

As Bolton observed, Chino labored "for nearly a quarter century (1687-1711), with headquarters at Mission Dolores, [and] founded missions in the San Miguel, Magdalena, Sonoita, Santa Cruz, and San Pedro valleys. A score of present-day towns began as missions that he established. He was the pioneer cattleman of the district, for in all these places he made the beginning of live stock raising."

Chino built more than thirty churches and missions, some of which remain to this very day. What is more, he recorded his activities and published several maps of the western territory—especially of California, which, he proved to be a peninsula, not an island.

Thanks to another Italian missionary, Father Salvaterra

40

EXPOSICION
ASTRONOMICA
DE EL COMETA,

Que el Año de 1680. por los meſes de
Noviembre, y Diziembre, y eſte Año de 1681. por los meſes
de Enero y Febrero, ſe ha viſto en todo el mundo,
y le ha obſervado en la Ciudad de Cadiz,

EL P. EUSEBIO FRANCISCO KINO
De la Compañia de Jesvs.

Title page, *Exposicion Astronomica de el Cometa,* by Francisco Chino.

from Milano who established the famous Pious Fund, the Chino missions continued to prosper and to multiply. Today, travelers to California cannot help but visit and enjoy the "chinian" hospitality.

ENRICO TONTI (1650-1704): *Born in Gaeta, Italy; Died in Illinois*

According to the *American Dictionary*, "tontine" refers to a "scheme in which subscribers to a common fund share an annuity with the benefit of survivorship, shares of the survivors being increased as the subscribers die, until the whole goes to the last survivor." Enrico Tonti, from whose name "tontine" is derived, was a Neapolitan banker who introduced this financial scheme to the French. "Tontine" has now become a universal banking term.

Enrico Tonti, however, deserves even greater recognition for other accomplishments, especially those he achieved in America while working for France. (One is tempted to recall Verrazzano's efforts in behalf of that nation, and how little recognition he has received.)

Henry de Tonty, as he is occasionally identified in American history books, came to America with La Salle's expedition of 1679. La Salle returned almost immediately to France, leaving Tonti in charge of what was then a vast, unexplored land comprising the entire Mississippi valley.

Tonti was among the first to explore Lake Erie and the Niagara region. He also established French colonies in many areas of Louisiana and Illinois, among them the center that was eventually to develop into the city of Chicago. For twenty or more years, he traveled through the Mississippi region, leaving the "Tontica"—large and small settlements scattered through the area—behind him.

In Italy, Tonti had built himself an artificial hand, having lost his own right hand in a military venture. Known throughout the Mississippi valley as "the man with the iron hand," he had a great reputation for skill in battle, and an unusual influence on the Indians. They admired him, however, as much for his humanity as for his strength. His colleagues likewise loved and respected him.

A modest man who chose not to boast about his many accomplishments, he is considered the true founder of Illinois, and the father of Arkansas as well. It should be known,

43

Enrico Tonti (from bas-relief by Edward Kemeys).

however, that Enrico was not the only Italian to work for France. His brother, Alfonso Tonti, co-founded Detroit and ruled over the territory for ten years. His son, Charles Henry Tonti, became a highly regarded soldier in the French-Canadian forces.

PHILIP MAZZEI (1730-1816): *Born near Florence; Died in Pisa*

Philip Mazzei was a man of various significant interests. He traveled throughout Europe and America, leaving behind unmistakable imprints of his own huminity, which had been nurtured by the great Italian culture. Every powerful sovereign sought Mazzei's presence and his services: he went to Turkey, England, France, Germany, Poland, and most important, the American colonies. There he became friend and consultant to George Washington, Thomas Jefferson, James Madison, Benjamin Franklin, Patrick Henry—with whom he marched against the British—George Mason, Payton Randolph, Benjamin Harrison, and many others.

Long before Thomas Paine published his inflammatory treatise, *Common Sense,* Mazzei was contributing to the Virginia and Pennsylvania gazettes and other local papers, making scathing attacks against the English tyranny. It was Mazzei, too, who challenged in person the Anglican ministers who had been sent to dissuade the colonists from taking up arms. If he was instrumental in bringing about American independence, he also made invaluable contributions toward the formation of American democracy.

A naturalized American citizen, he had originally come to Virginia to introduce the Italian agricultural system, and introduced many varieties of plants and wheat germs. But unlike the owners of the Africa Company of London, who became wealthy through their "inhuman and infamous traffic" (slavery), Mazzei devoted so much time and energy to his new country's political affairs that his own business practically failed. He observed:

After having stayed several days to talk with Jefferson about various things, but above all on the· subject to cooperate toward the formation of a good government, I returned to Albemarle with Bellini, and although I absented myself very little from my house, I was more taken up with the affairs of the country than with those of my own. (Memorie, pp. 227, 228).

46

Regarding "the formation of a good government," Mazzei helped to introduce Cesare Beccaria's humanitarian philosophy, which pervades such documents as the Declaration of Causes (1775), the Declaration of Independence (1776), the Constitution, and the Bill of Rights.

Mazzei himself worked on and translated the Declaration of Causes. Regarding the Declaration, Benjamin Franklin wrote in a letter to Mazzei (December 25, 1775):

> The Congress have not yet extended their view much towards foreign Powers. They are nevertheless obliged by your kind offers of your service, which perhaps in a year or two more may become very useful to them. I am myself much pleased, that you have sent a Translation of our Declaration to the Grand Duke; because having high esteem of the Character of that Prince, and not of the whole Imperial Family, from the accounts given me of them by my friend Dr. Ingenhouse and yourself, I should be happy to find that we stood well in the opinion of that court. (Memorie, pp. 232-233).

Mazzei's services did indeed become useful: he was the first official state diplomat to travel to Europe in behalf of the newly established United Colonies.

It was Mazzei, then, more than any other man, who brought to the colonies the spirit of the great Italian leaders and political philosophers. What follows is, in a nutshell, the philosophy that he imparted to the colonies:

> . . . to attain our goal it is necessary, my dear fellow citizens, to discuss the natural rights of man and the foundations of a free government. . . . All men are by nature equally free and independent. . . . The division of society into ranks has always and will always continue to be a very serious obstacle to the attainment of this end. . . . Democracy, I mean representative democracy, which embraces all individuals in one simple body, without any distinction whatsoever, is certainly the only form of government under which a true and enduring liberty may be enjoyed. (Marraro, p. v)

Unfortunately, most American founding fathers either could not or would not accept Mazzei's counsel: "The division of society into ranks has always and will always continue

Philip Mazzei: "Colonial patriot, helped finance American Revolution. Physician, author, botanist." (From the Victoria Mint.)

Dichiarazione
ei Rappresentanti delle
Colonie unite dell'America
settentrionale adunati in
Congresso Generale in Filadelfia, che espone le ragioni
della loro necessità di
prender l'armi

Se fosse possibile per uomini ragione-
voli di credere che il Divino Au-
tore della nostra esistenza avesse
voluto che una parte del genere uma-
no possedesse un assoluto illimitato
dominio sulle persone e sulla roba
delle altre / destinate dalla sua
infinita bontà e sapienza a por-
tar un duro e pesante giogo, al quale
non fosse lecito di opporsi / gli
Abitanti di queste Colonie potreb-
bero almen pretendere dal Parla-
mento della Gran Brettagna
qualche prova dell'essere stata
concessa a Lui questa tremenda
autorità sopra di esse. E la
la reverenza dovuta al nostro gran
Creatore, i principj d'umanità
e il senso comune, convinceranno
chiunque rifletta su tal soggetto,

... che sia ricominciata, ...
prima.

Con umile speranza nella
misericordia del supremo imparzial
Giudice e Regolatore dell'uni-
verso, devotamente imploriamo la
sua Divina bontà a volerci felice-
mente condurre al fine di questa gran
contesa, a disporre i nostri Avversarj
a riconciliarsi con condizioni ra-
gionevoli, e conseguentemente
a sollevar l'Impero dalle calamità
d'una guerra civile.

Per ordine del Congresso
Giovanni Hancock Presidente
Carlo Thomson Segretario

Filadelfia 6. Luglio 1775.

Mazzei's translation of the Declaration of Causes, first and last pages.

to be a very serious obstacle. . . ." Although Jefferson, among others, did want to free the slaves outright, England itself stood in the way: she had vetoed two laws aimed at freeing the slaves.

Mazzei proposed an alternate law that obliged "the slave owners to send young blacks to public schools to teach them reading, writing, arithmetic, and the art of making good use of liberty," rather than to free them outright, with neither means of survival nor the knowledge needed to participate in the democratic process. Much as John Adams felt exhilarated for having helped to free a poor wretch from execution, Mazzei reflected joyfully in his *Memorie* (p. 235) on the law he was instrumental in having passed: "the number of blacks that attained liberty from their owners increased with each day that passed."

CESARE BONESANA BECCARIA (1738-1794): *Born and died in Italy*

Harvard Professor Ernest II. Wilkins observes that "The influence of Beccaria's thought is manifest in the American Bill of Rights." When one thinks of the issues surrounding the first ten amendments of our Constitution, and if one understands Beccaria's little book, *On Crimes and Punishments*, one would not doubt Professor Wilkins' remarks.

A thorough study of the works of Beccaria, together with the Declaration of Causes, The Declaration of Independence, the Constitution, and the Bill of Rights, would prompt another observation that will surely upset many scholars of American history: without Beccaria, the United States would not have its present form of government.

Beccaria can be credited with two basic principles: governments have to be created to exist for the people; and a person is innocent until proven guilty. He can also be credited with the development of legislation concerning such subjects as established religions, freedom of speech and of the press, self-incrimination, secret accusations, and cruel and unusual punishments. Ample historical evidence to prove these statements can easily be found in the writings of John Adams, Thomas Jefferson, and many other Americans of this period.

Adams quoted directly from Beccaria as early as 1768, again in 1770 at the notorious trial following the Boston Massacre. Further, he quoted Beccaria in English and in Italian. Finally, he willed Beccaria's book to Thomas B. Adams, his son. (This copy, with John Adams own notations, is to be found in the Rare Book Department of the Boston Public Library; and all quotations from Beccaria appearing here have been taken from Adams' book.)

Thomas Jefferson was also inspired by Beccaria's humane philosophy. Jefferson's bills for proportioning crimes and punishments, his ideas regarding the separation of church and state, and his laws against the establishment of orders of nobility surely have their roots in Beccaria's own thought.

51

Cesare Beccaria (from an early print).

A N

E S S A Y

O N

CRIMES and PUNISHMENTS:

BY THE

MARQUIS BECCARIA, OF MILAN.

WITH A

COMMENTARY,

BY

M. DE VOLTAIRE.

A NEW EDITION CORRECTED.

In rebus quibufcunque difficilioribus non expectandum, ut quis fimul, & ferat, & metat, fed preparatione opus eft, ut per gradus maturefcant. BACON.

PHILADELPHIA:

PRINTED BY WILLIAM YOUNG, NO 52, SECOND-STREET, THE CORNER OF CHESNUT-STREET.

M,DCC,XCIII.

Title page: "An Essay on Crimes and Punishments: By the Marquis Beccaria, of Milan. With a Commentary, By M. de Voltaire." From a Philadelphia edition.

Concerning "proportioning crimes and punishments," Jefferson quoted from Beccaria as many as twenty-six times.

In one draft of the Declaration of Independence, Jefferson had written, "life, liberty, and property." For the final edition, he wrote, "life, liberty and the pursuit of happiness" —a principle utilized by Washington in his inaugural address to the first Congress of the United States of America. Beccaria had said that the single most important goal of any government is to assure "the greatest happiness of the greatest number."

The Preamble of the United States Constitution reads: [We the People of the United States, in Order to form a more perfect Union, establish Justice, insure domestic Tranquillity, provide for the common defence, promote the general Welfare, and secure the Blessings of Liberty to ourselves and our Posterity, do ordain and establish this Constitution for the United States of America.[

For the contents of the Preamble, our founding fathers owe more to Beccaria than most people are willing to acknowledge.

Most European governments of the time were monarchies bent on destroying any and all forms of republics. They were supported by structures based on family units and of constituted orders. The common citizen was not counted. The expression, "We the People," was therefore as alien to the Europeans as any other ideology that spoke on behalf of the single citizen.

In his chapter, "Of the Spirit of Family in States," Beccaria concerns himself with the procedures for governing large land areas and large numbers of people. He says:

It is remarkable, that many fatal acts of injustice have been authorized and approved, even by the wisest and most experienced men, in the freest republics. This has been owing to their having considered the state, rather as a society of families, than of men. Let us suppose a nation composed of an hundred thousand men, divided into twenty thousand families of five persons each, including the head or master of the family, its representative. If it be an association of families, there will be twenty thousand men, and eighty

54

thousand slaves; if of men, there will be an hundred thousand citizens, and not one slave.

During Beccaria's lifetime, the European governments —with the exception of the Republic of Venice and a few others—were despotic and centralized. Regardless of its form, monarchy—from the "absolute" in France, to the "enlightened" in England—was a bane to any republican form of government. For the Americans to want to establish a republic, therefore, was revolutionary to say the least. To want to establish it over a territory whose land size was bigger than all of Europe must have been mind boggling. The key to how they accomplished both—and here the Revolution can be distinguished from the War of Independence— may be credited to Beccaria:

An overgrown republic can only be saved from despotism, by subdividing it into a number of confederate republics. But how is this practicable? By a despotic dictator, who, with the courage of Sylla, has as much genius for building up, as that Roman had for pulling down. If he be an ambitious man, his reward will be immortal glory; if a philosopher, the blessings of his fellow-citizens will sufficiently console him for the loss of authority, though he should not be insensible to their ingratitude.

Thus, "We the People of the United States" may have its genesis in the work of an "Italian founding father."

Until the Constitution was drafted, Beccaria was perhaps more widely known and read in America than the contemporary philosophers of the Enlightenment. Voltaire was first published in America because of Beccaria.

According to the *National Union Catalog Pre-1956 Imprints*, Voltaire as an author was first published in 1778. His more important works did not appear until 1796, nine years after the Constitution was signed and five years after the Bill of Rights went into effect. Rousseau was first published in America in 1796, and Montesquieu not until 1802. On the other hand, Beccaria was being read in the Italian and English editions. More important, he was being published throughout the colonies.

In New York, the Rivington *Gazetter* advertised Beccaria's book as "in press," October 1773. In Philadelphia, it was published in 1776. In South Carolina, it appeared in 1777. A second edition was published in Philadelphia in 1778. Other editions appeared subsequent to the 1770 decade.

The same book, *On Crimes and Punishments*, was first published in Leghorn, Italy in 1764. By 1770, it had been translated and published in many editions throughout Europe. Adams' copy, for instance, had been published in England.

Cesare Beccaria became famous also for other works. To have an idea, it suffices to quote directly from *Webster's Biographical Dictionary*:

[Beccaria . . . Italian economist and jurist . . . Professor of law and economy . . . anticipated in his lectures economic theories of Adam Smith, and theories of Malthus on population and subsistence . . . Author of Tratto dei Delitti e delle Pene (1764), which condemns confiscation, capital punishment, and torture, and advocates prevention of crime by education; his ideas had widespread effects, influencing Catherine II of Russia and the French revolutionary code.]

Beccaria's popularity was perhaps mainly due to the honesty and simplicity with which he discussed issues such as capital punishment, secret accusations, gun control, public prayer, crime prevention, abortion, political crimes, and many other issues which are as alive in the twentieth century as they were during the decade of 1770.

John Adams, Thomas Jefferson, Philip Mazzei, George Washington, and others drew strength from Beccaria's writings as they worked to resolve certain fundamental issues. Beccaria's works continue to be published; and the vigor of his mind and judiciousness of his intellect may yet give guiding strength to the men and women of the Equal Rights era.

WILLIAM PACA (1740-1799): *Born and Died in Maryland*

William Paca was the only signer of the Declaration of Independence who was not of Anglo Saxon ancestry. Although his signature is among the most clearly written—"Paca," not "Parker"—he is rarely identified in our history books or other works dealing with his period. Yet if one reads the *Jefferson Papers* and the accounts of Dickinson, the name Paca stands out: he was instrumental in getting the rough drafts and the final rendition of the Declaration through the several committees, whose members often opted to guard personal interests rather than those of the nation about to be born.

Many have claimed that Paca was not of Italian descent. Nevertheless, in a letter to *The New York Times* (July 8, 1937), Mr. W. S. Paca of Chestertown, Maryland, confirmed that William was the grandson of Robert Paca, who came to America by way of England, settling in Maryland, where he was granted a 490-acre tract in Anne Arundale County. Giovanni Schiavo refers to an article published in the *Baltimore Sun* (July 3, 1904) which states that in Italy Robert Paca married the daughter of a commissioner who had been appointed by Oliver Cromwell. Out of this marriage came a son named Aquila (in English, it translates, "Eagle"), who became high sheriff in Maryland.

It is reasonable to assume that Robert named his only son Aquila in honor of the boy's Italian grandparents on his mother's side. The Aquilas, like the Paccas, were a prosperous south-Italian family. Aquila had a son and named him William.

William is a descendent of the Paca family of Benevento and Naples. Several men of the family became famous. One was a cardinal in the church. Another was Nicola Aniello Pacca, the famous Neapolitian historian of the sixteenth century.

We know that William Paca, himself, was a successful lawyer. He was also the first governor of the state of Mary-

William Paca: "Maryland's first Governor and Supreme Court Justice. Signer of the Declaration of Independence." (From the Victoria Mint.)

land (1782-1785), and a United States district judge for Maryland (1789-1799).

FRANCIS JOSEPH VIGO (1747-1836): *Born near Torino; Died in Indiana*

Within the museum of the Statue of Liberty, a painting and a taped monologue pay tribute to Colonel Francis Vigo. Because the Statue of Liberty has been a symbol of hope for millions of immigrants, whose physical, intellectual, and creative efforts have helped to build America, it is entirely fitting that this museum has chosen to recognize a great Italian-American. The Statue of Liberty, incidentally, was sculpted by Bartholdi, a Frenchman of Italian parentage.

Like the millions of immigrants who came after him, Francis did not know how to read or write. He enlisted in a Spanish rifle company in Cuba and subsequently came to New Orleans. After a noteworthy military career, he became an immensely successful fur trader. He was able to amass his fortune not simply because he was a shrewd businessman, but also because he understood the Indians' ways: he spoke their language and respected their culture. As a result, he was accepted and recognized as a friend and a great man wherever he went.

In 1779, Vigo placed himself at the service of General George Rogers Clark to wage war against the British. Vigo enlisted the necessary soldiers, and provided for their pay and subsistence. At Vincennes, which was heavily fortified by the British, Vigo allowed himself to be taken prisoner. After he had studied the enemy's defense plan, Vigo escaped with the aid of his Indian friends.

The resultant battle saw the Americans victorious. America acquired the Northwest Territory—Illinois, Ohio, Indiana, Wisconsin, and Minnesota, the largest plot of land in the history of the world to be acquired through a single battle. The State of Indiana has established Vigo County in recognition of this feat.

Take any common textbook on the history of America, and most likely, you will not find Vigo's name. He appears in neither Bailyn, Becker, Crane Brinton, Hazelton, nor De Voto. C J. Richards, however, recognizes Vigo as unique

Francesco Vigo: "Patriot, fur trader. Army officer under George Rogers Clark. Helped to finance the War of Independence." (From the Victoria Mint.)

in the history of America. Considering the wealth that Vigo accumulated entirely for the sake of his country (he died, poor and forgotten) our history books would do well to remember this Italian colonel of the Northwest Territory, who fought alongside General Clark. Vigo was one American who gives meaning to the late John F. Kennedy's injunction: "Ask what *you* can do for your country."

LORENZO DA PONTE (1749-1838): *Born in Treviso; Died in New York*

Emanuele Conegliano—or Lorenzo Da Ponte, as he is known in the world of music and the arts—is another eighteenth-century Italian who traveled the world, leaving behind distinct traces of Italy's humanistic culture.

Born and raised in Ceneda, outside of Treviso, Lorenzo was an ordained priest and lived in Venice for an extended time. Because of personal difficulties, he left the lagoon city and went to Gorizia. Finding no peace in the new place, he went to Dresden, Germany and then to Vienna, where he was to make a great contribution to the world of music.

Living in the famous Austrian city, he wrote several librettos for opera, three of which have been immortalized by Wolfgang Amadeus Mozart. *The Marriage of Figaro* (1786); *Don Giovanni* (1787), and *Cosi Fan Tutte* (1790) have been enjoyed the world over, both for the felicitous music and the measured lyrics. Many critics consider these three operas to be Mozart's masterpieces.

Da Ponte came to the United States by way of Holland and London, where he found himself in serious difficulties: he fled to Philadelphia in 1805, and eventually went to New York. In America, as in Europe, he lived a vagabond life, teaching Italian, establishing academies, and selling books.

He also brought together the Montresor Company of Italian opera, which opened at the Richmond Theater in New York (1832). The Company also performed at the Chestnut Street Theater in Philadelphia the following year. Unfortunately, Da Ponte wrote no new librettos for the Montresor Company; and he never discovered the talents of an American Mozart.

When he lived in New York, Da Ponte petitioned the trustees of Columbia College for permission to teach Italian. They agreed to allow classroom space, but refused to pay him a salary. Nevertheless, Da Ponte conducted classes in Italian language and culture until his death. He never received a cent from the college, but made a meager living from the

63

Lorenzo Da Ponte: "Librettist for Mozart poet, Columbia University professor. Founded first N.Y. Italian Opera House." (From the Victoria Mint.)

"reasonable compensation" he received from his students.

Thanks to Peter Riccio, Columbia University established its Casa Italiana in 1972. Perhaps Da Ponte's initial work was not all in vain.

BENJAMIN TALIAFERRO (1750-1821): *Born and Died in Georgia*

It is not uncommon to read in our history books about the soldier Esteban, who was killed leading the first Spanish exploration into Arizona and New Mexico (1539); but few, if any American books mention Marco da Nizza and Friar Oronato in conjunction with the famous expedition into Arizona. We also read about the Indian woman Sacajawea, who served as guide and interpreter on the Lewis and Clark expedition into the Northwest Territory (1804); but little is said about Francis Vigo, who made possible the conquest of that territory. History has similarly ignored the Taliaferro family, although the men and women bearing this name have played important roles in America's development.

The Taliaferro were active citizens since the very beginning of American history. Among the most outstanding were Benjamin and Richard. Benjamin, who during the Revolution was captain in the Rifle Corps commanded by General Morgan, later became president of the Georgia senate, and attended the sixth and seventh congresses of the United States.

Like William Paca, who was chief justice in Maryland, Benjamin was a judge in the Georgia Superior Court. The state of Georgia remembers him with the city of Taliaferro (located northwest of the city of Augusta), much as Canada remembers Burlamacchi with the city of Burlemaque.

Richard Taliaferro, a famous Virginia architect in the 1770 decade, was a colonel in the War of Independence. He was a member of a committee elected to enforce the Association in the James City County. He died in the battle of Guilford Hall (March 15, 1781); and his name is recorded in the famous monument to Major Winston, located in Greensboro, North Carolina.

Francis Taliaferro Brooke (son of Ann Hay Taliaferro and Richard Brooke) later became a general. Another Taliaferro, Elizabeth, married George Wythe of Virginia, one of the signers of the Declaration of Independence. The family

Benjamin Taliaferro: "Patriot, congressman, judge. Served as captain in Revolution. Representative from Georgia in U.S. House." (From the Victoria Mint.)

also contributed two officers to the Civil War: Captain W. T. Taliaferro, and General W. B. Taliaferro.

Taliaferro ranks among the oldest American names. The name, in its original form, remains prominent to this day; and one wonders also about the derivation of such names as Talifer, Tolovar, and Telfair. Several members of the family have recently graduated from Harvard University. The name is also well known among the top financial executives of the business and art worlds. Surely, this American family of Italian descent has helped America to become the great nation it is today.

GIUSEPPE CERACCHI (1751-1802): *Born in Rome; Died in France*

Giuseppe Ceracchi created in sculpture the good likenesses of several American patriots of the revolutionary period. In the decade of 1790 alone, he completed statues of George Washington, Thomas Jefferson, John Jay, James Madison, John Paul Jones, George Clinton, David Rittenhouse, and possibly thirty others. At this time, he also collaborated with William Rush and Charles W. Peale to help found what today is known as the Pennsylvania Academy of Fine Arts.

Perhaps Ceracchi's most important work, however, is his statue of Alexander Hamilton. John Trumbull painted his famous portrait of Hamilton directly from Ceracchi's bust; and a photograph of this portrait appears on the cover of the West Suburban Boston Telephone Directory (special bicentennial edition, 1975-1976), with credit given to "Giuseppi Ceracchi" inside. Trumbull also painted a portrait of Ceracchi, himself, which now hangs in the Art Gallery of Yale University.

Like his compatriots Vittorio Alfieri (who wrote the first ode to celebrate America's war of independence) and Ugo Foscolo (the famous Italian poet who wrote against tyranny) Giuseppe Ceracchi was a political idealist of the Age of Enlightenment. All three men had faith in Napoleon Buonaparte and his promises of liberty. (Even Beethoven had fallen for the Italian-born general). They were disappointed, however, when Napoleon terminted the free Republic of Venice and turned Italy into a quasi-province of France, and when he crowned himself Emperor of a people who had fought a revolution in behalf of freedom.

An ardent soldier in liberty's behalf, Ceracchi followed his conscience and turned against the Emperor. Apprehended in a plot against Napoleon's life, Ceracchi was sentenced to the guillotine. We do not know if he was in fact beheaded, or if he died in jail, insane.

We do know, however, that he had come to America with

Trumball's painting of Alexander Hamilton (from Ceracchi's bust).

the intention of erecting a 100-foot statue to the Goddess of Liberty—a plan he was never to fulfill. The Statue of Liberty, itself, was later to be sculpted by another artist of Italian lineage, Frederic August Bartholdi. But Ceracchi's influence on Getulio Piccirilli, who directed the carving of the statue of Lincoln for the Lincoln Memorial, is unmistakable.

Ceracchi, interestingly enough, depicted many of the American founding fathers in traditional Roman garb, even though he was able to carve in every historical style. Did Ceracchi think that the Roman ideal of a Republic had finally been achieved—in America.

ALESSANDRO MALASPINA (1754-1810): *Born in Mulazzo; Died in Pontremoli, Italy*

In his days of glory, Alessandro Malaspina may not have heard of Bobadilla's chains. In his days of degradation in Spanish jails, he must have found solace thinking about the fate of his earlier compatriot, Christopher Columbus, the Universal Admiral. Malaspina may have even envied Captain James Cook.

Hardly twenty years old, Alessandro graduated from the college of Palermo and immediately joined the Spanish fleet. By the time he was twenty-seven, he had circumnavigated the world; and at thirty-five he was a captain in the Royal Navy, commanding two custom-built corvettes, *Atrevida* and *Descubierta*. In 1789 he set sail with these two ships, embarking upon the scientific career that was to bring him to the western coast of South and North America, all the way to Alaska and the Bering Sea, and down to the Philippines, New Zealand, and Australia.

In five or more years of arduous scientific research, Malaspina laid plans for the excavation of the Panama Canal, showing the feasability and utility of such an undertaking. He measured the height of Mount Saint Elias in Alaska, exploring the gigantic glaciers that were later named after him. Working out of Acapulco, he fixed the measurements of America's western coast with a precision never before achieved. In Ecuador, he measured the Chimborazo, one of South America's highest peaks. He also gathered geodedic, botanical, and mineral information, and produced many maps of places unknown to the civilized world.

Upon his return to Spain, Malaspina ran afoul of Godoy, minister to Charles IV, and—after so many years of glorious service to His Catholic Majesty—was sentenced to spend six years in a Spanish jail. He was freed only through the intercession of Napoleon in 1802; but it was too late for the Italian scientist, explorer, and navigator to continue his remarkable activities. A good part of his scientific collection was dispersed or lost in the land which he had brought so much glory.

72

Alessandro Malaspina (by an unknown artist).

SALVATORE CATALANO (1771-1846): *Born in Sicily; Died in Washington*

Perhaps the greatest tribute paid to Salvatore Catalano was the United States Navy's order that he be made pilot of the frigate, *Congress*, and of the world-famous "Old Ironsides," the U.S.S. *Constitution*. "Old Ironsides is now on display in the Boston Harbor, thanks to the efforts of Oliver Wendell Holmes, whose poem about the ship has stirred the hearts of Americans of all ethnic backgrounds. Thanks, too, are due to Joseph Fondecaro for his skillful work in the restoration and preservation of the venerated naval unit.

Salvatore Catalano, however, is to be remembered alongside Commodore Edward Preble, Lieutenant Stephen Decatur, and William Eaton, all of whom were responsible for America's naval victory against the Arab corsairs of the Barbary Coast. Fighting thousands of miles away from American shores, the United States Navy gained worldwide recognition as a naval power, thanks to the help given by this young Sicilian sailor.

The Barbary pirates played havoc with the European shipping lanes until Jefferson grew tired of paying ransom money: in 1799 the Americans had bought peace from Algiers and Tunis for $800,000, and were supplying annually one frigate plus $25,000. The president sent out a squadron of ships; and stirred by such slogans as "Millions for defense but not one cent for tribute," American vessels engaged the pirates in their own waters.

Executing a wrong manoeuvre, the Americans ran their ship aground. The pirates quickly seized the *Philadelphia* and turned it into an impregnable floating fortress. Unwilling to accept defeat, Commodore Preble secured the services of Catalano, and made him the pilot of the ship, *Intrepid*. Under cover of darkness, the Sicilian brought the vessel within range of the captured ship. The American sailors quickly boarded it, battled the pirates, and set the *Philadelphia* aflame. This battle made it possible for America to secure peace with Tripoli on June 4, 1805.

In his report to Commodore Preble, Decatur made the

Salvatore Catalano: "Piloted the *Intrepid* under Stephen Decatur into battle. Later pilot of 'Old Ironsides.'" (From the Victoria Mint.)

following statement: "It would be unjust in me, were I to pass over the important services rendered by Mr. Catalano, the pilot, on whose good conduct the success of the enterprise in the greatest degree depended."

GIACOMO BELTRAMI (1779-1855): *Born in Bergamo; Died in Florence, Italy*

Recently described in *American Heritage* magazine as the "flamboyant" explorer and adventurer, Beltrami sought to discover the source of the Mississippi. He was acknowledged by a Minnesota Legislature proclamation (1866) as the discoverer of the source of the most famous American river.

Come to America by way of Liverpool, England, Beltrami, a former magistrate in the Napoleonic government, received permission from General Clark to join his military forces stationed at the fork of the Mississippi and Minnesota rivers. The historian Imperatore reports that Beltrami made several incursions into the area to study the geography and the customs of the local Indians.

After having joined another military expedition which explored the American territory along the Canadian border, Beltrami decided to go out on his own. With two Indian friends (who soon abandoned him) he set out to reach Red Lake, which feeds the Thief River Falls. Toward the end of August 1823, after several days of wandering, Beltrami came upon a small lake—the source of the Mississippi River, which he named Lake Julia.

Having accomplished this feat almost singlehanded, Beltrami set out southward traveling as far as Mexico. On this journey he explored the countryside and made accurate geographical observations. He also made several archeological observations to prove that the "new world" was not necessarily newer than the "old world."

Schiavo tells us that Beltrami published an account of his discoveries in New Orleans. Back in London, he published his famous two-volume work, *A Pilgrimage* (1828) which achieved immediate popularity. Such famous authors as F. R. Chateaubriand and James Fenimore Cooper have found in Beltrami's books background material for their own works.

Much as Vigo is remembered in the name of Vigo County,

A .

PILGRIMAGE

IN

EUROPE AND AMERICA,

LEADING TO

THE DISCOVERY

OF

THE SOURCES OF THE MISSISSIPPI

AND BLOODY RIVER;

WITH A DESCRIPTION OF

THE WHOLE COURSE OF THE FORMER,

AND OF

THE OHIO.

By J. C. BELTRAMI, Esq.

FORMERLY JUDGE OF A ROYAL COURT IN THE EX-KINGDOM OF ITALY.

IN TWO VOLUMES.

VOL. I.

LONDON:
PRINTED FOR HUNT AND CLARKE,
YORK STREET, COVENT GARDEN.

1828.

Title page: "A Pilgrimage in Europe and America, Leading to the Discovery of the Sources of the Mississippi and Bloody River; With a Description of the Whole Course of the Former, and of the Ohio. By J.C. Beltrami, Esq. Formerly Judge of a Royal Court in the Ex-Kingdom of Italy." From Giovanni E. Schiavo, *Four Centuries of Italian-American History.*

Indiana, Giacomo Costantino Beltrami is remembered in the name of Beltrami County, Minnesota. Thanks to the Italian city of Bergamo, the state of Minnesota owns an oil portrait of the famous explorer. Beltrami, without a doubt, is a fitting subject for those artists and writers interested in early America.

CONSTANTINO BRUMIDI (1805-1880): *Born in Rome; Died in Washington, D.C.*

Brumidi, who came to the United States in 1852, brought with him the glorious Italian art of fresco painting. His frescoes decorate the many walls and cupolas of our national Capitol Building.

Brumidi was a student at the Roman Academy of Fine Arts and the Academy of San Luca. He studied sculpture under the Danish-Italian, Bertel Thorvaldsen, and under the famous Antonio Canova. He also studied painting under Maestro Camuccini. Among his earlier achievements, Brumidi restored Raphael's Vatican Loggia.

He was also a captain in the military services. As the result of a disagreement with the Vatican Guards, who had enlisted him for further service, Brumidi was imprisoned. With the help of Pope Pius X, he was soon released and decided to leave Italy.

In America, he stayed for a brief period in New York before proceeding to Mexico City. There, he executed important works of art for which he became famous.

Brumidi was eventually recalled from Mexico and given a small commission to work on the decoration of the United States Capitol Building. From 1852 until his death, he worked in the manner of Michelangelo, imparting beauty and meaning to many areas of the building. The frescoes of Cornwallis asking for a truce (in the Statuary Hall) and *The Apotheosis of Washington* (in the canopy of the Rotunda) are Brumidi's work. He also depicted in fresco *The Death of General Wooster*, and did portraits of his fellow Italians, Christopher Columbus and Americo Vespucci, as well as John Fitch, William Brewster, and others.

Brumidi's death in February, 1880 resulted from an accident on a high scaffold in the Capitol rotunda. It is said that he was left dangling for about six hours before being rescued; and by that time, he was too badly injured to recuperate. Like many of his fellow countrymen, Brumidi died in poverty and without recognition.

Constantino Brumidi: "Artist and sculptor, chosen by Jefferson. Known as 'Michelangelo of the U.S. Capitol.'" (From the Victoria Mint.)

SAMUEL MAZZUCCHELLI (1806-1864): *Born in Milano; Died in Benton, Wisconsin*

He was "Father Kelly" to the English-speaking Catholics of the North Central States. In Wisconsin, Iowa, Ohio, Michigan, Illinois, and Ottawa, Canada—Father Mazzucchelli traveled the entire area—Indians and white settlers alike knew him as a friend and teacher.

He was only twenty-one years old when he came to America in 1828. After having spent several months in France, he came to Cincinatti, and was ordained a priest two years later. From then on, Mazzucchelli was the veritable indefatigable missionary. Among his many contributions, he translated a catechism into the Winnebago language, and published an almanac in the Chippewa language.

He is known for his architectural contributions. He built about twenty churches, some of which still stand. One, the Church of Saint Augustine, erected in Wisconsin in 1844, is now preserved as a national monument by the Knights of Columbus. Another, the Church of Saint Gabriel, is still being used by a parish, according to Judith Kleinmaier.

A Dominican, he founded the Order of the Dominican Sisters of the Holy Rosary. He also built schools, among them the Sinsinawa Mound College for Men, where he served as first president and teacher.

Father Mazzucchelli is also credited for having designed Iowa's Capitol Building, the Iowa State University, and the Bishop's Residence in Dubuque. The state legislature held its first session in one of Mazzucchelli's churches. In Wisconsin, he was asked to open the First Territorial Legislature with a prayer.

Mazzucchelli was not the only Italian to help with the exploration and settlement of the vast American territory. Wherever they went, Italian missionaries introduced Christian ideals and secured their perpetuation, building numerous churches and schools for the benefit of future generations.

Mazzucchelli, like Sister Bentivogilo and Father De Andreis, is now being considered by the Vatican for sainthood.

Fr. Samuel Mazzuchelli: "U.S. missionary. Built 30 churches &
schools in midwest. Designed Iowa state capitol." (From the Victoria Mint.)

Should they to be canonized, the number of Italian-American saints would come to four.

ANTONIO MEUCCI (1808-1889): *Born in Florence; Died in New York*

In almost every major reference publication in Italy, Antonio Meucci is recognized as the inventor of the telephone. The Italians, to cinch this claim, state that the United States Supreme Court decided thus, in favor of Meucci and against Alexander Graham Bell. Research, however, reveals no such court case, and no such decision. Yet Meucci does seem to be the first (and legitimate) inventor of the telephone.

Having left Florence as a young man, Meucci landed in Cuba, where he worked as an electrician at the Tacon Opera in Havana. When the Opera House burned down in 1850, Meucci came to America and settled in Clifton, New Jersey, where he established a prosperous candle factory.

There he collaborated with the famous general, Giuseppe Garibaldi, experimenting with a gadget that would transform sound waves (produced by the human voice) into electrical impulses—an idea with which Meucci had been preoccupied since he was fifteen years old. He accomplished the first voice telephone transmission in 1857. Unfortunately, this achievement generated interest neither among friends nor professional colleagues.

In 1871, Meucci took his invention to the Patent Office in Washington, D.C., for a caveat. In 1876, Alexander Graham Bell took his invention to the same office and received a patent. Two hours after Bell had presented his invention, Elisha Gray presented his own invention for a caveat, but did not receive the award.

After having received his caveat, which is similar to a patent, Meucci approached Mr. Grant, then president of the New York Telegraph Company, and gave him the documents relevant to the new invention. Meucci returned to Mr. Grant several months later, only to learn that the documents had been lost. The Globe Telephone Company, however, did buy or secure from Meucci the rights to manufacture his telephone.

The Bell Company brought suit against the Globe Com-

85

Antonio Meucci: "Supreme Court ruled he invented telephone before Alexander Graham Bell." (From the Victoria Mint.)

pany and won. The Western Union Company then appealed Judge Wallace's decision against the Globe Telephone Company; and it was during this period of appeal that Meucci unfortunately died. The Supreme Court was called into the case when the Western Union Company, which had been constructing telephone instruments on Meucci's caveat, was sued by the Bell Telephone Company; and perhaps the court should then have decided once and for all who the real inventor was. As it happened, however, the two companies suddenly turned friends and settled out of court: the Bell Company paid Western Union an amount exceeding one million dollars.

It should be added that both Alexander Bell and Elisha Gray, the third among many contenders to the invention of the telephone, had their offices and laboratories in the Western Union Building; and it was supposedly over Western Union wires that two electricians, Prescott and Pope, tested Meucci's telephones. Prescott and Pope had been in contact with the same Mr. Grant who had received—and conveniently lost—Meucci's documents, instruments, and drawings.

Those who would like to see justice accomplished according to the best American traditions might want to read *Antonio Meucci, Inventor of the Telephone*, by Giovanni E. Schiavo. Although Judge Wallace and a few others believed Meucci to be a fraud, many others who have studied the documents will not hesitate to observe that a greater fraud may have been perpetrated on an Italian immigrant who came to America to fulfill his dreams. However, the time may not yet be ripe to vindicate Meucci's name.

EUGENIO VETROMILE (1810-1880): *Born and Died in Gallipoli, Italy*

Eugene, as he was known among the inhabitants of Maine, came to America in 1840 and settled in Washington, D.C. He became a student at Georgetown University, where he studied for the religious life. Ordained a priest, he assumed duty as a missionary, first at Fort Tobacco, Maryland, then in Old Town, Maine (1858), where he lived among the Penobscot Indians, to whom he dedicated his life. He finally returned to his native Gallipoli, in southern Italy, just in time to die.

If Vetromile performed his religious duties with all proper attention, his passion lay in the field of linguistics. He was particularly interested in the languages spoken by the Penobscots and other Indians in the north-eastern United States. According to the Reverend Edward Ballard of Brunswick, Maine, "He was the only one who could read and understand the translated verses of John Eliot's Indian Bible."

Father Vetromile published several volumes about his travels in Europe, Egypt, Palestine, and Syria; but his most famous works were those about the American Indians: the *Aln'amby Uli Awikhhigan,* a volume of devotions and instructions in the various Abnaki dialects; the *Ahiamihewomtunghangum, a collection of hymns set to music; the Vetromile Wewessi Ubidian,* an Indian Bible, and the *Abnaki Dictionary.*

Father Vetromile is only one of the hearty Italian missionaries to work throughout the American land, from California (Chino and Salvaterra) to the Northwest Territory (Father Mazzucchelli) to the hills of the northeast. They preached the word of God, leaving behind works of rare dedication. The American Indians' true friends were often Italians: Francis Joseph Vigo, Alessandro Malaspina, the Tonti brothers, Constantino Beltrami, Fathers Tosi, da Nizza, and others. What we have today in the form of treaties and linguistic studies was largely due to the efforts of Italian settlers and missionaries.

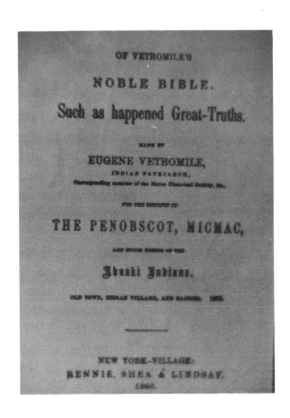

Title Page: "Of Vetromile's Noble Bible. Such as happened Great-Truths. Made by Eugene Vetromile, Indian Patriarch, Corresponding member of the Maine Historical Society, As, for the benefit of The Penobscot, Micmac, and other tribes of the Abnaki Indians. Old Town, Indian Village, and Bangor. (Date unintelligible.)"

ANTHONY RAVALLI (1811-1884): *Born in Ferrara; Died in Spain*

"Laboring to the last despite the feebleness of years," reports the *National Cyclopedia of American Biography*, "Ravalli was the ideal missionary—patient under suffering, simple, affectionate, and physically robust. His reputation in the Rockies, won through forty years of hardship, was second only to that of De Smet."

A Jesuit missionary among the Indians, Father Ravalli worked towards the necessary goal of bringing religion and civilization to the Wild West—to what are now the Rocky Mountain States. He arrived in Vancouver, British Columbia in 1884, and soon went into the Montana territory to live among the Kalispel and Colvilles Indians. He quickly mastered their language, and earned a reputation among them for his skill in medicine. He also worked in northern Idaho, where he built a flour mill, a sawmill, and a church, whose altar piece he carved himself. For a brief period, Ravalli left the wild country to serve his order at Santa Clara College, then returned to dedicate his life to the Indians and the hundreds of European miners scattered throughout Montana.

Ravalli was only one of many Italian men and women who helped transform the American wilderness. Chino, da Nizza, and Salvaterra, who explored the new land on Spain's behalf; Vetromile, who worked among the Penobscot Indians in Maine; Sisters Tommasini, Trincano, Segale, and Bentivoglio, and of course, Mother Cabrini—these Italian missionaries have contributed amply to America's growth.

It is therefore no surprise that the American landscape is dotted with hundreds of churches, monasteries, schools, and hospitals, founded if not built by the very hands of these hard-working people. Yet in these very schools, the study of Italian language and culture is rare indeed.

Examining Schiavo's superlative history of the Italian Americans, one is awed to learn just how much the Italian missionaries accomplished: Anthony and Philip Filicchi

Anthony Ravalli (from the *New Catholic Encyclopedia*).

helped Mother Seton to establish the Order of the Sisters of Charity. Father Giovanni Grassi transformed a small school into what is now Georgetown University, and served as its first president. In Missouri alone, Bishop Rosati built thirty-four churches, the Cathedral of St. Louis, and various colleges, academies, orphanages, and hospitals. Other institutions of higher learning were also established: the University of Santa Clara, by Father Accolti; the University of San Francisco, by Father Maraschi; Woodstock College, by Father Angelo Paresce; Gonzaga College, by Father Cataldo; and St. Bonaventure's College in New York, by Father Pamphilus.

Ravalli, then, was not alone; nor were the Jesuits the only ones who were active: Franciscans, Dominicans, and Scalabrini were all working toward one goal—to Christianize the Wild West through dedicated hard work. It is no surprise, in light of these efforts, to discover that Mazzucchelli, de Andreis, and Bentivoglio are now being considered for cannonization.

LUIGI PALMA DI CESNOLA (1832-1904): *Born in Piemonte; Died in New York*

Before he came to the United States, General Palma was already famous throughout Europe as an archeologist and diplomat. During his tenure as the Italian consul in Cyprus, he became interested in the ancient history of that island, and participated in archeological excavations there. Fortunately for the United States, he collected the Cypriote Antiquities, then worth about $200,000, and eventually arranged for the collection to be purchased, for about $60,000, by the newly founded Metropolitan Museum of Art.

If the Metropolitan Museum has become all that it is today, much of the credit must go to this Italian, the museum's first director. (The Louvre Museum in Paris, incidentally, is similarly indebted for its greatest expansion to an Italian, Catherine de Medici.) Palma worked feverishly to collect works of art and to expand the museum building, and succeeded in giving America what is perhaps its richest artistic resource.

This, however, was no easy task. From 1879, when he became director, until his death, he was opposed and persecuted. Antagonists denigrated the artists, and fought against the establishment, maintenance, and embellishment of the prestigious museum. The attacks were so frequent and vicious that at one point, Cesnola lost his temper and struck back angrily, incurring a lawsuit for libel. He was acquitted after a three-month-long trial that became famous throughout the United States.

Luigi Palma had the pioneer spirit that impelled him to continue with his work. Upon his death, he was recognized by such men as Carl Schurz and Pierpont Morgan.

In an editorial dated December 3, 1904, the *Scientific American* paid Palma the highest tribute: "The Metropolitan Museum of Art, as we know it today, may be regarded as a monument to his energy, enterprise, and rare executive ability."

Few people know, however, that prior to his election as

93

Luigi Palma de Cesnola: "Won Medal of Honor in Civil War. Made a General by Lincoln. First Director Metropolitan Museum." (From the Victoria Mint.)

museum director, Palma had served with distinction in the United States Army. He had received the Congressional Medal of Honor; and President Lincoln had promoted Colonel Palma to the rank of brigadier general. Surely, in the person of Luigi Palma di Cesnola, Generals Thaddeus Koseiusko and Serge Koussevitzky have a brother-in-arms who has yet to be sufficiently recognized.

BANCROFT GHERARDI (1832-1903): *Born in Louisiana; Died in Connecticut*

Gherardi was one of two Italian-Americans of the Civil War period to be recommended by the United States Congress for promotion to the rank of rear admiral.

For forty-one years, from the time he received orders to serve on the U.S.S. *St. Louis* until his last assignment in 1893, Commander Gherardi distinguished himself as a naval officer. He was a commander in the North Atlantic, and a military diplomat in the settlement of the Haitian Revolution. As a shore officer, he commanded navy yards in the Philadelphia, Mare Island, and New York areas. He was also governor of the Naval Asylum and president of the Naval Examining Board.

His father, Donato Gherardi, had immigrated to the United States in 1825. He settled in Jackson, Louisiana where he taught Latin and Greek at the Round Hill School. There he met and later married Jane Bancroft, sister of George Bancroft, the famous American historian. Young Gherardi was named after his famous uncle.

In 1872, Commander Gherardi married Anna Talbot Rockwell of San Francisco, with whom he had two sons. One son, Walter R. Gherardi, followed in his father's footsteps, becoming a rear admiral himself, and commanding the Boston Navy Yard.

Rear Admiral Bancroft Gherardi saw service on many ships: the *Ohio, Sarana, St. Louis, Saratoga, Lancaster, Chippewa,* and the *Mohican.* He commanded the ships *Chocura, Port Royal, Richmond, Independence, Colorado, Pensacola* (flagship of the North Pacific Squadron) and *Lancaster* (flagship of the European Station). He saw action during the bombardment of Alexandria, and distinguished himself in the Battle of Mobile Bay.

Admiral Gherardi was one of the many officers of Italian descent in service of the Union Army. There were Major General Edward Ferrero, who saw action in the second battle of Bull Run; Brigadier General Francis Spinola, who

96

Bancroft Gherardi: "Rear Admiral, headed U.S.N. Exam Board, U.S.N. Asylum, & New York Navy Yard." (From the Victoria Mint.)

was twice wounded at the battle of Wapping Heights; Brigadier General Luigi Palma di Cesnola, who was awarded the Congressional Medal of Honor and later became the director of the Metropolitan Museum of Art of New York; and Brigadier General Enrico Fardella, who saw service at Plymouth, North Carolina. There were also nine colonels, six majors, twenty-two captains, thirty-two first lieutenants, twenty-one second lieutenants, four surgeons, and four chaplains.

Richard S. Von Schriltz, an authority on the Civil War, mentions the following Italian units: Grenadier Regiment, Line Cavalry Regiment, Bersagliere Regiment, Light Cavalry Regiment, Military Mounted Police, Military Foot Police, Lancer Regiment, and the Line Infantry Regiment. He also mentions the Mounted Carabinieri (from Monaco, which at that time belonged to Italy); the Malta Royal Artillery (from Malta); the Line Infantry Regiment and the Noble Guard (from San Marino); the Mounted Gendarm Escort, the Pope Officials, the Noble Guard Escort, and the Papal Dragoons (from the Vatican).

Among those who helped to preserve the Union, Italian Americans did not hesitate to do their share of duty—a duty that continued through the first and second world wars, when the Italian Americans proved once and for all their patriotic allegiance to this great land, America.

ADELINA PATTI (1843-1919): *Born in Spain, Died in Great Britain*

Adelina Patti's voice set America and the world afire. She was perhaps the first great operatic *diva* to live and work in the United States.

Adelina's father was a well known tenor from Catania, Sicily; and her mother was an accomplished soprano from Rome. She was born in Madrid where her father was on tour, and under her parents' influence, grew up to absorb all that the theatre had to offer. She gave her "first debut" in New York at age seven, singing the aria, "Una voce poco fa . . ." from Rossini's *Barber of Seville*. During her childhood, she gave concerts throughout the world, learning to speak and read the languages of the different countries in which she performed: Italian, French, Spanish, German, English, Russian, and Roumanian. She also became a writer, and a composer of music in her own right.

Not quite seventeen, she was back in New York, performing at the Academy of Music. On November 24, 1859, her debut in Donizzetti's lyrical opera, *Lucia di Lamermoor* was a clamorous success. Historians of music still refer to that evening as the one that ushered in "the reign of Patti."

Giovanni Schiavo, historian of the Italian-Americans, observes, "Students of the history of opera need not be reminded of the furor that Adelina Patti created during the following forty-six years . . . until 1906, when she retired from professional singing. Both in Europe and in America she had become a legend. Traveling throughout the United States in a private railroad car which is said to have cost $60,000, her earnings during three seasons from 1882 to 1885 reached the fabulous sum of $450,000."

America has felt the musical impact of Frank Sinatra, the Beatles, and Elton John. And still one has to wonder if anyone reigned so long and as consistently as Adelina Patti.

99

Adelina Patti: "Greatest operatic 'diva' of her era at the Metropolitan. 'Queen of Song' made debut at 16." (From the Victoria Mint.)

Mother Cabrini: "Founder of schools, orphanages and Missionary Sisters of Sacred Heart. First American Canonized as a saint." (From the Victoria Mint.)

SAINT MARIA CABRINI (1850-1917): *Born in Italy; Died in Chicago*

Maria Francesca Saverio Cabrini is a saint in the truest sense of the word. In her lifetime, she was known as the "vagabond of Christ" and the "mother of the immigrants." Yet, she was a tiny woman, charged with tremendous spirituality and humanity.

Maria achieved many things during her lifetime. She founded the Missionary Order of the Sacred Heart of Jesus. She opened schools for children from families who could not afford adequate schooling. She founded the grandiose Columbus Hospital of New York, and built a chain of hospitals throughout the United States (on her deathbed, she had plans for still another such hospital). She opened orphanages throughout the world, and organized what are known today as day care centers.

She worked among the poor in Europe; and in the United States she concentrated her efforts in such cities as New York, New Orleans, Chicago, Philadelphia, Denver, and Los Angeles. New York City remembers her with Cabrini Square.

Maria visited destitute Italian immigrants wherever they were, bringing them comfort and the word of God. She went into plantations, deep mines, factories, jails, and hospitals, learning about her countrymen, who in turn appreciated and benefited from her presence. She gave them the strength, courage, and hope they needed to prevail over the dire conditions in which they were living and working.

In 1950, the Saint Frances Xavier Cabrini Order of the Missionary Sisters was operating fourteen colleges, ninety-eight schools, twenty-eight orphanages, eight hospitals, four dispensaries, three training schools for nurses, four ambulance services, six day nurseries, two rest homes, and two preventoriums.

Mother Cabrini became a naturalized American citizen. In her, the United States of America has its first saint—and what a saint, all will agree.

FRANCIS HORACE VIZETELLY (1864-1938): *Born in England; Died in New York*

Francis was the son of Henry Richard Vissetelli, one of the founders of the famous *Illustrated London News*. Henry Vissetelli was largely responsible for the publication of the works of Emile Zola, the father of French Realism whose parents, incidentally, were of Italian ancestry. For this contribution, Henry encountered such persecution that in 1891 young Francis Vizetelly had to move to America, where he undertook his family's trade. He was soon to be recognized alongside Webster as the champion of the "American" language—that is, of English as it was spoken and written in the United States. It was not until 1926, however, that he became a citizen of this country.

Recognized as one of the world's foremost lexicographers, he was a major contributor to many publications. He was editor of several magazines and reference works: *Home and Country Magazine*, the *Annual Cyclopedia*, *Woman's Home Companion*, *The Merck Index*, the *Columbian Encyclopedia*, the *Cyclopedia of Classified Dates*, the *Jewish Encyclopedia*, the *Schaff Herzog Encyclopedia of Religious Knowledge*, the *Cyclopedia of Practical Quotations—English and Latin*, the *Literary Digest*, *Lexicographer's Easy Chair*, the *Mental Efficiency Series*, the *Desk Book of Errors in English*, the *Dictionary of Simple Spelling*, *How to Use English*, *Our Color Box of Speech*, the *New Standard Encyclopedia of Universal Knowledge*, the *New International Year Book*.

Francis Vizetelly received many honors during his lifetime of relentless work, including an honorary LL.D. degree from Saint John's College. Knighthood was conferred upon him by the Order of Francis Joseph of Austria Hungary.

Perhaps the greatest tribute to Vizetelly was made in the *National Cyclopedia*: "He was an ardent defender against English critics, of the American language, with all its slang and colloquialisms, and of the American accent asserting that by reason of its vitality, directness and independence, American speech was superior to the British."

Francis H. Vizetelly (from the *National Cyclopedia*).

ARTURO TOSCANINI (1867-1957): *Born in Parma; Died in New York*

Maestro Toscanini is regarded by many as the greatest conductor of all time. Unlike Enrico Caruso, who died at an early age, Toscanini lived a long, active life, bringing credit both to himself and the world of music.

A tailor's son, Toscanini graduated from the Parma Conservatory of Music at age eighteen. He played cello in many orchestras, including one that took him to Rio de Janiero, Brazil. There the local director, who had quarreled with the Italian musicians and singers, refused to lead the program. Toscanini took over, leading the musicians in a memorable performance.

Toscanini was always received enthusiastically. He directed many orchestras, and conducted the debut performances of several operas: *Otello, I Pagliacci, La Boheme,* and others. He spent several years with the La Scala Opera House, but was also affiliated with the New York City Metropolitan Opera and New York's Philharmonic Symphony Orchestra. The National Broadcasting Company Orchestra was assembled especially for him.

In all his years of performance, Toscanini was never to direct with the score in front of him. He remembered every aspect of the music, and never made mistakes.

According to the Maestro, there is only one interpretation to any given score—the composer's. As a result, he revolutionized the interpretive art of the conductor: Beethoven, for instance, had to sound like Beethoven—the music of *all* the great composers had to sound exactly as *they* would have wanted.

Toward the end of his vigorous life, the Maestro searched for someone to take his place. In 1948, he discovered the talents of Guido Cantelli. As Toscanini's protege, the young Cantelli was introduced to America, and in no time was recognized by music lovers as a great conductor in the tradition of the Maestro. In fact, Cantelli also conducted from memory.

105

Arturo Toscanini: "World's greatest conductor of Opera and Symphony for over 50 years. His genius made America first in music." (From the Victoria Mint.)

In 1956, en route to New York, Guido Cantelli was killed in an air disaster. The news of his death was deliberately kept from the aging Maestro, who died the following year. Thus, the world lost two musical giants in less than one year.

MARIA MONTESSORI (1870-1952): *Born in Chiaravalle, Italy; Died in Holland*

Although Maria Montessori was the first woman in Italy to become a physician, graduating with a double degree in medicine and surgery, the world remembers her most for her contributions to the field of education. She is responsible for the most significant revolution in education since the Renaissance humanists overturned the scholasticism of the Middle Ages.

Education, observes Reginal Orem, international exponent of the Montessori system, "consists of helping the child's normal expansion during the critically important early years, by enhancing the child's physical, emotional, intellectual, social, and spiritual development." The Montessori method, Orem points out, aims at a comprehensive approach to the child's education, working towards the prevention of defects rather than at their costly, untimely, and often ineffective remediation.

Modern schools from Boston to San Francisco, with all their remedial programs, might benefit from the precepts put forth by Maria Montessori. A mentally and physically healthy child, she observed, is a good student; and a poor student is often a sick child. It is therefore necessary to communicate with children when they are still young, looking out for the warning signs of future intellectual or emotional disorder, and working to prevent problems *today*—not tomorrow when it will be too late.

The goal of education, then, has to be the child; and whatever part or parts are needed by an educational system must always be a means to the child's ends. The system has to prepare the proper environment, and make available not only an array of didactic materials, but teacher-type observors as well.

In the traditional system, the role of the teachers remains constantly strong. In the Montessori system, the focus on the teacher diminishes as the child expands and matures. Away with traditional classroom format, in which teachers

108

Maria Montessori: "Originated Montessori Method of pre-school teaching used in U.S. Italy's first female physician." (From the Victoria Mint.)

impart "knowledge" to rows of immobilized listeners who are not allowed to experience directly and for themselves the real joys of learning!

Maria Montessori was a great lady. Children were her concern because she worshipped *life*!

AMADEO PETER GIANNINI (1870-1949): *Born and Died in California*

"Amedeo," not "Amadeo," is the most common Italian version of Giannini's first name. Stamp collectors will remember him in connection with the recent United States Commemorative that honors this famous banker.

The word "bank" comes from the Italian "banco"; and "bankruptcy," from "bancarotta." Giannini is one of many great men of finance to emerge from the system, originating with the Florentines of the early Renaissance, that has given the world the banking institution and the modern form of accounting. It is no wonder, then, that an Italian should have founded the largest banking establishment of all time.

The son of Italian immigrants, Giannini established a branch of the Bank of Italy in San Francisco as early as 1904. Making liberal and favorable loans available to small businessmen and farmers, he became prosperous and successful. After the San Francisco earthquake and fire, Giannini utilized his capital to rebuild the city.

He established regional branch banking in 1909, when he opened the San Jose branch of the Bank of Italy; and within one year, this new bank doubled in size. In 1938, he organized the Transamerica Corporation, which he consolidated into the Bank of America National Trust and Savings Association. By 1948, he had succeeded in giving America and the world the largest single banking institution (over 500 branches), with assets exceeding six billion dollars.

Before his death in 1949, Giannini had already given away more than half the value of his enormous estate. Today, the Bank of America continues to bring credit to the Giannini family, to America, and to the world of banking.

A.P. Giannini: "Founder Bank of Italy, Bank of America. World's largest financial institution." (From the Victoria Mint.)

Enrico Caruso: "Hailed as world's greatest tenor. Mastered and excelled in entire Italian operatic repertoire." (From the Victoria Mint.)

ENRICO CARUSO (1873-1921): *Born and Died in Naples, Italy*

In the words of George Jellinek, Enrico Caruso "was one of the most famous, influential, and best-loved singers of all time. His artistry represented a clear departure from the old-fashioned school of vocalism in which beautiful tone and technical agility were all-important; he blended them with a human warmth and an instinctive dramatic sense to create a superbly harmonious whole."

Before coming to the United States, Caruso had studied voice for several years with Guglielmo Vergine and Vincenzo Lombardi. He had his debut in 1894 at the Teatro Nuovo of Naples, and quickly became known throughout Italy. He achieved his first big success in a premier performance of Giordano's *Fedora*, given at the Teatro Lirico of Milan. Later, he signed with La Scala, and rose to international prominence in less than two years.

In London, New York, and many other famous cities, he sang in French and Italian operas: *La Boheme, Othello, Les Huguenots, Carmen, Rigoletto, Aida, Tosca*, and many others. At the Metropolitan Opera House, he sang over 600 times, and was the audience's favorite opening-night tenor for sixteen years. During this time, he made about 250 recordings which are available in today's international catalogs: listening to his arias from *I Pagliacci* and *Cavalleria Rusticana*, one can still appreciate his voice and marvel at its range.

Recently, the great artist and art expert Giovanni Castano was asked why Caruso's legend lingers. Gastano answered that Caruso was not great because of his voice alone, but because of his great soul. And that is the way it must be.

114

ANGELO B. ZARI (1873-1956): *Born in Pisa; Died in New York*

The thousands of people each year who visit the Lincoln Memorial, the Tomb of the Unknown Soldier, and the Marine Memorial—all in Washington—can all see that the greatest human ideals have been made tangible in the architectural and sculptural forms realized by this Italian immigrant from Pisa. The list of Zari's projects, accomplished by himself alone or in collaboration, is impressive: the New York Public Library, the Pan American Exposition buildings, the Hotel Pennsylvania, the Central and Bowery Savings banks, the New York Academy of Medicine, the Pershing Square and Graybar buildings, the approaches to the Holland Tunnel, Temple Emanu-El, the Arlington Memorial Ampitheater, the National Gallery of Art, the National Archives Building, the Pan American Union Building, the Seals of the States of the Union, the Statler and Olympic hotels, the state capitol buildings of Pennsylvania and Missouri, the Delaware River Bridge, Convention Hall of New Jersey, the Lincoln Memorial of Illinois, the Great Kills Marine Park of New York, the new wing for the New York Metropolitan Museum of Art, the Micro-Biological Building of Rutgers University, and many, many others.

Angelo Zari's great soul is reflected in his countless architectural forms, and in the many pieces of sculpture on display throughout America. One cannot help but feel awed by his many structural feats, and inspired by his statuary accomplishments.

That he received a gold medal from the Italian government for his contributions is hardly worth mentioning in view of the monuments he has left behind. More than for any other gold medal he could have received, Angelo Zari should be remembered as one who "did things" rather than "talk things." For this, every American of whatever origin can be grateful and justly proud.

The extent of Zari's accomplishments, however, should be no surprise, considering the traditions of Italian archi-

115

Angelo B. Zari (from the *National Cyclopedia*).

tecture, sculpture, and painting from which he emerged! Other great Italian architects are Pier Luigi Nervi, who won two gold meals in the late 1960's; Andrea Palladio, without mention of whom one cannot discuss Bulfinch's Washington Monument or Washington D.C., itself; Giacomo Quarenghi, who built the most significant edifices in Moscow and Petersburg; Bartolomeo Rastrelli, who built churches and palaces, not to mention the Hermitage Museum in Russia; Rossi, who built Russia's Ministry of War; Trezzini, who built Russia's Summer Palace; Filippo Terzi, whose name is synonymous with Lisbon's architecture; and last but not least, the little-known Girolamo Veroneo, reputedly the architectural designer of India's famous Taj Mahal.

Guglielmo Marconi: "Scientist, inventor of the wireless telegraph. 1909 winner, Nobel Prize in Physics." (From the Victoria Mint.)

GUGLIELMO MARCONI (1874-1937): *Born in Bologna; Died in Rome*

Guglielmo, or William Marconi, should perhaps be considered the father of the Age of Communication, just as Marco Polo, another Italian, is the father of the Age of Exploration.

Guglielmo was the son of an Italian father and an Irish mother, Annie Jamison. The two nationalities combined to produce a genius. In another instance, the same nationalities produced Charles Siringo, who fathered the literary tradition of the cowboy. Siringo's book, *A Texas Cowboy*, sold over a million copies.

Marconi studied first in Leghorn and then in Bologna. His teacher, the famous scientist Augusto Righi, had already done considerable work in the field of electromagnetism. Other great scientists of this period were Volta, Ampere, Faraday, Maxwell, Hertz, and De Forest, who is considered by many to be the inventor of the radio. It was Marconi, however, who excelled in the field of radio communication.

In 1896, he built the first wireless transmitter. He modified this instrument so that in the following year he was able to transmit coded messages back and forth between France and England. In 1901, he transmitted in code between England and the United States; and in 1903; the *London Times* was receiving coded messages from the United States for its daily news coverage.

Marconi's fame was established, and he received the Nobel Prize in 1909. Nobel Prizes have also been conferred upon Fermi (atomic energy), Bovet (physiology), Segre (physics), and Natta (chemistry).

One year after he received the Nobel Prize, Marconi established communication networks between Europe and South America. Finally, in 1927, he succeeded in transmitting the human voice, itself: two people—one in England and one in Australia—spoke to each other by means of Marconi's radio transmitting system.

Today, some fifty years later, we can engage multiple and simultaneous transmissions on earth; we can land men on the moon, effect outer-space rendezvous, and explore the infinite universe. The man whose communication system helped make this possible was rather humble and of good nature, glad to have contributed to human progress through his great inventions. He is truly deservant of the epithet, "father of the Age of Communication."

JOSEPH FACCIOLI (1877-1934): *Born in Milano; Died in Massachusetts*

An expert in the field of electricity, Joseph Faccioli researched, improved, and developed new machinery to generate and transmit an alternating electric current. Educated in Italy, he is yet another Italian-American whose efforts have contributed to the growth of his adopted country.

Having solved many problems pertaining to high-tension electrical transmission, Faccioli pioneered in the development of the corona system first used in eastern Colorado, as well as the high-tension switching and line oscillations used in the systems of the Great Western Power company. His experiments led to the development of high-tension transformers, lightning arresters, and protective equipment.

According to the *National Cyclopedia*, Faccioli "did what William Stanley considered pioneer work in forecasting by method of calculation the results which would be obtained on a new type of alternating-current generator." The Italian-born engineer was therefore invited to work as Stanley's chief assistant in Great Barrington, Massachusetts. Stanley's works became part of General Electric in 1907; and in 1927, Faccioli was named engineer and associate manager of that company's electric works in Pittsfield, Massachusetts.

Faccioli was responsible for organizing the American Institute of Electrical Engineers, and bringing that group up from the local to the national level. He also wrote many scientific articles that were published in contemporary journals. Upon his retirement in 1930, the Institute awarded him the famous Lamme Medal for his achievements, scholarly contributions, and political leadership in the electronics field. Surely, Faccioli's accomplishments distinguish him not only as an outstanding Italian-American, but also a worthy citizen of the world.

Like many inventors—among them, Bellaschi of Westinghouse—Faccioli emerged from a long line of Italian scientists who worked with electricity. Alessandro Volta (as in "watts and volts") made numerous discoveries in England, France,

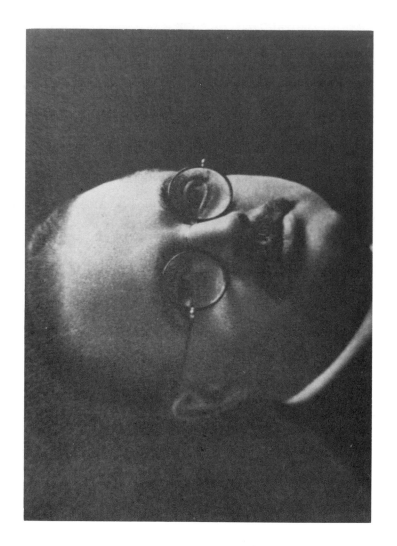

Joseph Faccioli (from the *National Cyclopedia*).

and Russia. The battery, which, like Marconi's radio, we use everyday, was one of Volta's inventions. Luigi Galvani, from whose name comes the word, "galvanize," discovered that electricity can be produced by chemical action. Antonio Pacinotti was the first to discover how to use electromagnetism to turn a dynamo—that is, to convert electricity into power. Galileo Ferraris discovered the rotary magnetic field. And we must not forget Giulio Natta, the recent Nobel Prize winner, who through his research in plastics has developed and patented a motor that runs on energy from the sun.

FIORELLO HENRY LA GUARDIA (1882-1947): *Born and Died in New York*

Fiorello is one of the most colorful figures in American political history to appear at the city and congressional levels.

The son of an army bandmaster, Fiorello grew up in Arizona. At the age of sixteen, he traveled to Budapest, Hungary, and later to Italy where he was employed at the United States consulates in Trieste and Fiume. Back in America, he worked as an interpreter for the United States immigration service while studying law at New York University. He was admitted to the Bar in 1910; and six years later, he was elected to Congress as a Republican. He resigned from Congress soon afterwards to serve as pilot in the Air Force, then under the auspices of the United States Signal Corps.

He returned to Congress after completing his military tour of duty. During this time, he also served as president of the New York Board of Aldermen. In 1922, he co-sponsored a bill with Norris that forbade courts to issue restraining injunctions against strikes, boycotts, or peaceful picketing. In 1933, he was elected mayor of New York City.

Fiorello governed the city for almost ten years, during which time, he was known as the "little flower." He was a reform mayor in the traditional Italian humanitarian manner, fighting corruption, fostering civic improvements, and bringing about a revision of the city's charter. Many people

People remember him fondly: for all his flamboyance, Fiorello was one of the few mayors to cope with New York City's many problems. Until recently, he was the only Italian-American mayor to govern a large city.

Before he died, he was director of the Office of Civilian Defense, and director general of the United Nations Relief and Rehabilitation Administration.

As Italian-Americans become more aware of the challenges presented by America's political system, more leaders of Fiorello's calibre are surely to come forth to fill the gap left since his death.

Fiorello H. La Guardia: "Dynamic New York mayor 1934-1945. Energetic, colorful leader dedicated to betterment of mankind." (From the Victoria Mint.)

Henry Woodhouse (from the *National Cyclopedia*).

HENRY WOODHOUSE (1884-1919): *Born in Torino, Italy; Died in America*

Enrico Casalegno—or Henry Woodhouse, as he is known to the aeronautics world—was already an expert linguist, economist, and sociologist when he came to America in 1904. By the time he became a naturalized citizen in 1909, he had written numerous articles for leading journals of his day. Eventually, he founded *Flying*, today's foremost magazine on aviation, and the weekly magazine, *Aerial Age*. He also founded the National Aeroplane Fund, the Patriotic Education Society, and the Aeronautics Federation of the Western Hemisphere.

Among those who strove for a strong, independent America, Henry Woodhouse was an ardent advocate for a strong national defense. To support this cause, he founded the Patriotic Education Fund. He was a member of other national-defense organizations, and was the permanent delegate to the Conference Committee on National Preparedness.

He supported actively the efforts of Glenn H. Curtis, the American inventor and pioneer aviator. Woodhouse also championed the cause of research in his many articles and speeches, and more importantly, with his generous subsidies.

In 1912, he urged the employment of airplanes as postal carriers. He also made a study concerning the possible deployment of airplanes in combat missions. His observations, however, were too advanced for his time: only today have Americans begun to appreciate the aeronautical ideas first promulgated by this immigrant from Torino.

The name Woodhouse brings to mind yet another field where men and women of Italian lineage—among them, the late Joseph M. Bellanca—have worked and achieved for the benefit of all Americans. Woodhouse is to surface flight aviation what Rocco Petrone—the present head of NASA, under whose leadership American space vehicles have landed on the moon—is to outer-space exploration.

Joseph M. Bellanca (from the *National Cyclopedia*).

JOSEPH M. BELLANCA (1886-1960): *Born in Sicily; Died in New York*

In the history of aviation, a few important events merit our remembrance: the maiden flight of Orville Wright in 1903; the first crossing of the Atlantic by Lindbergh in 1927; and the second crossing by Levine one month later; the crossing of the Atlantic with ten hydroplanes by Balbo in 1931, the establishment of the still-unbroken world record for speed (709 kilometers per hour) by F. Agello in 1934; the development of the Caproni-Campini jet plane in 1949; the flight by Gloster and Whittle, of the Frank Whittle turbojet in 1941; the breaking of the sound barrier by Charles Yaeger in 1947; and the development of various rocket families, derived from the first motor-driven plane of Wilbur and Orville Wright.

Italians, among them Henry Woodhouse (Enrico Casalegno) and the great Secondo Campini, have participated in this great avionic adventure both in Italy and the United States. Vitally important, too, were the contributions made by the great airplane manufacturer, Joseph M. Bellanca.

In 1907, Bellanca built a plane that would compete in the crossing of the English Channel. He had been studying at the Istituto Tecnico and Politecnico in Milan, and graduated in 1910 with degrees in engineering and mathematics. One year later, Bellanca emigrated to the United States; and in 1912 he established the Bellanca Airplane School.

He built three planes for the United States Post Office Department for use in the delivery of mail; and after having built the airplane, *Columbia* for the Wright Aeronautical Corporation, he decided to establish his own company. In 1927, the same year that Lindbergh was to cross the wide Atlantic, he created the Bellanca Aircraft Corporation.

During his lifetime, Bellanca greatly influenced the history of avionics. It was he who proposed that engines be placed in the front, rather than in the back of airplanes; and he introduced the air-cooled engine, which replaced the water-cooled

129

models. He designed the first closed planes, and won important races as early as 1922.

In June, 1927—one month after Lindy's famous flight—one of Bellanca's planes, piloted by Charles A. Levine and carrying one passenger, made a 3905-mile flight across the Atlantic. In 1931, Bellanca's plane was the first to make a non-stop, 4500-mile flight from Washington to Tokyo. This flight was accomplished in forty-one hours.

He built, among other planes, the famous *Tandem* (1930), the *Cruisair* (1948), and the *Cruisemaster* (1949). He also built bombers and fighters for the United States Air Force.

The Italians have contributed much more to the history of avionics than the helicopter design of Da Vinci. How unfortunate that the names of these brilliant, daring individuals have fallen into near-obscurity!

PETER A. YON (1886-1943): *Born in Torino; Died in New York*

The Triumph of St. Patrick is one of Peter Yon's most beautiful and best known musical works. Yon wrote the score for this famous oratorio (the text is by Armando Romano) while employed at St. Patrick's Cathedral in New York, where he was church organist for sixteen years. Yon's organ music, especially that written for the church, is played throughout the United States and Europe. Yet most people cannot determine from his name that Yon—like Walter Piston, another Italian-American composer—was of Italian lineage.

Peter Yon began his musical career at age six, in the city of Ivrea, which enjoys fame today as the home of the Olivetti-Underwood industry. There, he took lessons from Angelo Burbatti, the organist at the cathedral. Yon went on to the Milano Conservatory, the conservatory at Torino, and finally to the Liceo di Santa Cecilia in Rome, from which he graduated with honors in 1905. He then became assistant organist at St. Peter's Basilica.

In 1907, after having given many recitals in Europe and America, Yon immigrated to New York, where he became the organist at St. Francis Xavier's Church. He remained there for almost twenty years, playing and composing sacred music for the various religious events.

He became an American citizen in 1921, and in 1927 he was appointed organist at the famous St. Patrick's Cathedral on Fifth Avenue. Later, after the death of J. C. Ungerer, Yon became choir director. It was during his sixteen-year tenure at St. Patrick's that Yon wrote his most beautiful music, and performed his virtuoso concerts. " . . . by virtue of his position and talents," said Vernon Gotwalls, Yon was "the informal dean of Catholic church music for many years."

Yon died in 1943, at the height of a war involving Italy and the United States—a war whose tragic implications touched him deeply. The results of this war still weigh heavily on many consciences; and it is hoped that the situation will not be repeated. But as things are developing in the latter half

131

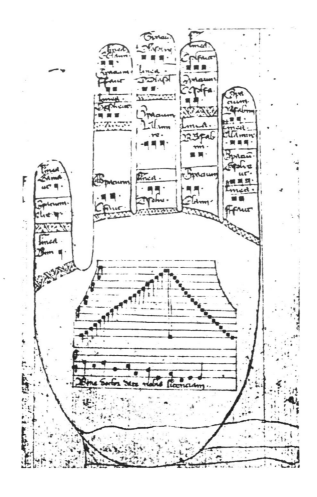

Ninth century: pentagram with seven notes, by
Guido d'Arezzo.   Guido invented the musical
scale, which, with one addition, has remained
unchanged. (From *Attraverso I Secoli*.)

of the 1970's, chances are that many more Italian-Americans will be forced to endure the same sort of tragedy so deeply felt by such men as Yon, Toscanini, and Salvemini.

Of Yon's hundreds of compositions, two are in Italian: *Gesu Bambino* and *Natale in Sicilia*. In *Gesu Bambino* (Baby Jesus), Yon underscores the tune of "Adeste Fidelis" ("Come All Ye Faithful"), which Italians sing throughout their beautiful land. The lyrics of this sacred song, however, must have been written in some strange language, for few modern Italians seem to understand their meaning or accept their message.

ANTHONY DE FRANCISCI (1887-1964): *Born in Sicily; Died in New York*

Italy has produced a more-than-ample share of sculptors; and Italian sculpture ranks with painting, music, architecture, and the sciences as a great contribution to western culture. If everyone has heard of Michelangelo, Bernini, Donatello, and Manzu, few of us know about the many Italian-American sculptors and painters whose works embellish the world's finest museums and public places.

America is certainly richer for the contributions of Anthony De Francisci, who came to America from Sicily in 1904. He was a sculptor who excelled in medallic and coin design: the 1921 silver dollar is among the more famous examples of his work; and veterans of World War II wear De Francisci's special commemorative button on their uniforms. He decorated monuments as the Independence Memorial in New York City, and the facade of the Federal Post Office in Washington, D.C.

De Francisci was an instructor at Columbia College and the Beaux Arts Institute in New York. He belonged to many organizations in different capacities, among them the Association of National Academicians, the American Numismatic Society, and the National Sculpture Society. His art, like that of other Italian-Americans, is on display in the more famous American and European museums.

Many Italian-American artists were born in the United States of Italian parents: Mary Maravigna; Theodore Barbarossa, whose works decorate the facade of the Boston Museum of Science; Rudolfo Corsini, who cast several medals for the series, *They, Too, Made Our Country Great*; and the all-but-forgotten Anthony Di Bono. Others, like De Francisci, were born in Italy and came to America at a yong age: Charles Pizzano, and Giovanni Castano, whose scenes of America are admired throughout our nation.

Italian-American sculptors produced thousands of pieces, which are to be found in churches, cemeteries, and public places. Many such treasures decorate the porticos of the

134

Anthony de Francisci: "Leading Fine Arts Sculptor of modern times. Designed 1921 U.S. Silver Dollar." (From the Victoria Mint.)

United States Capitol Building. The art is there, though the artist has too often been relegated to obscurity, as in the cases of Piccirilli and Bartholdi. Thanks to the historian Giovanni Schiavo, some of the names have been recovered: Caffieri, Medici, Ceracchi; Perovani, Cocchi, Rossetti, Bartoli, Pise, Iardella, Franzoni, Andre, Casoni, Causici, Valaperti, Cappellano, Persico, Fargnani, Corne, and many, many others. The Italian government, incidentally, commissioned the great Antonio Canova to sculpt a bust of George Washington.

WALTER PISTON (1894-1976): *Born in Maine; Died in Massachusetts*

The winner of two Pulitzer Prizes and one New York Critics' Circle Award, Walter Piston is known throughout the world as a distinguished modern American composer.

He was the grandson of Antonio Pistone, an Italian sailor who Anglicized his surname after he settled in Maine and married into an American-born family. Antonio's son (Walter's father) was a bookkeeper, and he moved his family to Boston when Walter was nine years old. There Walter, who studied violin, attended the Mechanic Arts High School where he played in the school orchestra. After graduation he studied at the Massachusetts School of Art; and during this period he earned his living playing violin and piano in various Boston-area dance halls.

After a stint in the Navy during World War I (the young enlistee was made Musician Second Class; and the band in which he played was stationed at the Massachusetts Institute of Technology), Walter entered Harvard University. There he conducted the university orchestra for three years, and graduated with honors in 1927. Years later, after composing innumerable pieces of music and making various tours of the United States and Europe, Walter returned to Harvard as a professor of music. In this capacity, report Rossi and Rafferty, "he taught two generations of composers (including Leonard Bernstein)."

Today, serious students of music cannot help encounter Piston's name. From 1933 until 1955, he wrote four textbooks that have been widely acclaimed: *Principles of Harmonic Analysis* (1933), *Harmony* (1941), *Counterpoint* (1947), and *Orchestration* (1955).

Among Piston's contemporaries were the composers Ives, Stravinsky, Copeland, Malipiero, Schoenberg, Bartok, Menotti, Varese, Prokofiev, Dello Joio, Barber, Respighi, Castelnuovo-Tedesco, Yon, De Sabata, and Persichetti. They participated in a "revivalist" period of music history that saw the emergence of many different forms: polytonality,

137

Walter Piston (from Rossi and Rafferty, *Music through the Centuries*).

atonality, pandiotonicism, primitivism, dodecaphonicism, and polyrhythmicism.

In the midst of all this upheaval, Walter remained basically a classicist, achieving international fame with such works as the *Suite for Orchestra* (1929), the *Incredible Flutist* (1938), the second, third, and seventh symphonies (1943, 1948, and 1961), and the *Violin Concert* (1960). His orchestral works have been performed under the direction of such world-reknowned maestros as Fiedler, Rodzinski, Zighera, Reiner, and Munch.

Walter spent the latter part of his life with his wife in Belmont, Massachusetts. (She, incidentally, fulfilled his own secret dream of becoming a successful painter; and it would be interesting to speculate to what extent the two artists influenced each other.) He remained a highly individualistic man, observing, at one point, "We already have a large literature of music by native composers. The outstanding characteristic noticeable in this music is its great diversity. If a composer desires to serve the cause of American music, he will best do it by remaining true to himself as an individual and not trying to discover musical formulas for Americanism."

Recalling the Pistonian humor, Edmund Brown, dean of Boston editors and longtime friend of Walter's, offers the following anecdote:

Walter lived in Belmont, but did not know much about his neighborhood. One day, on main street, a certain woman stopped him.

"Mr. Piston, I hope you don't mind my asking," she said, "but you don't seem to go to work much. What do you do?"

"Madam!" he answered somewhat perplexed, "I stay home as much as possible, trying to write music."

"I suppose that's as good a way of wasting time as any," she answered a smile, and continued on her way.

Poor Walter was left dumbfounded. Suddenly, he smiled and returned to his studio.

Rudolph Valentino: "Hollywood's top silent screen star of all time. Idol of millions as 'The Sheik'" (From the Victoria Mint.)

RODOLFO VALENTINO (1895-1926): *Born in Castellaneta, Puglia; Died in New York*

The great Valentino never spoke a word on screen, but he became the idol of movie-goers throughout the world.

His real name was Rodolfo Pietro Filiberto Guglielmi. Born in the little-known village of Castellaneta in the south of Italy, he lived in France as a boy, and eventually came to America. Like thousands of Italian immigrants who came to the "promised land," Rodolfo took any jobs he could in order to make a living. One day, unexpectedly, his fortune changed.

Rex Ingram, the famous silent-movie producer, discovered Rodolfo and cast him for a movie part. "Rudolph Valentino's" success was immediate: the idol of millions, he captured the public heart and imagination as few had done before him. Portrayed on screen as the archetypal Latin lover, he was actually a simple, noble man who had been deeply affected by the beautiful traditions of the 2000-year-old society of his birth. He believed in the *famiglia*—in all the family values that had been handed down through the ages. Could a man with this solid an upbringing survive amid the gaudiness, the fanfare, the money—all the artificial glories of Movieland?

Perhaps it was a blessing that death paid Valentino an early visit, as it had Enrico Caruso some five years earlier. The short lives of these two giants, however, live on in the legends they created through their talents, and more important, through their profound humanity.

Valentino made several memorable films, four of which shine out in the already glittering history of the early cinema: *The Four Horsemen of the Apocalypse* (1921), *Blood and Sand* (1922), *The Black Hawk* (1925), and *Son of the Sheik* (1926).

FELIX FORTE (1895-1976): *Born and Died in Boston*

In Phillip Mazzei and Thomas Paine, America had the two most effective non-American revolutionaries of the 1770 decade. The first expounded the humanitarian principles of Beccaria, the second, the "meritorious" principles of Dragonetti. Of the two, Paine was the more revolutionary: he had come from England—where the king was the law— to proclaim in America that law was king of the land.

"The law is king," a principle that has guided the United States for over 200 years, was threatened just once, when Nixon believed that as president, he was above the law. It fell on the shoulders of an Italian-American judge (Sirica) to re-establish our guiding principle, and an Italian-American congressman (Rodino) to secure obedience to Paine's statement.

Many may think it strange to hear Italian names cited in connection with such important events as the establishment of American government in the 1770's (Paca and Taliaferro), and the rescuing of that government from the vitiations of the Nixon era (Sirica and Rodino). The scholar of jurisprudence, however, remembers that Rome gave the western world laws that endured through the ages of empires and nations, and remain to guide modern societies. It is therefore no surprise to discover that modern Italians have emerged from this tradition to contribute to the legal and judiciary fields.

Paca and Taliaferro, Sirica and Rodino—they achieved special prominence, perhaps because there were crisis situations at hand to propel them into the spotlight. Yet there are other attorneys and judges of Italian descent—among them, Felix Forte—who have worked behind the scenes, quietly and with uncompromising vigor, in behalf of the American legal tradition.

Judge Felix Forte was one of many Americans of Italian descent to serve on the judicial system. Others have been Judges Re and Rao (U.S. Customs Court), Celebrezze (U.S. Court of Appeals), Zirpoli and Tauro (U.S. District Courts),

142

The Honorable Felix Forte.

Quirico, Scott, D'Ambrosio, and a score more. Any American president could have chosen among many Italian-Americans to serve on the Supreme Court.

Forte's parents immigrated to Boston from southern Italy. Young Felix displayed an aptitude for jurisprudence even as a student at Boston University, from which he graduated *cum laude*, and also received a master's degree. During his tenure as an advanced student at Harvard University, he taught law at Boston University, and was made full professor there in 1929. He received a doctorate in juridical science from Harvard in 1932.

Forte established a private law practice, and participated in a wide variety of activities: he was an officer of the Republican State Committee, and a Supreme Venerable of the Sons of Italy in Massachusetts. A witty, brilliant, and enlightened lecturer, Forte traveled throughout Europe and the United States to speak on the American judicial system. He received many awards, including an honorary degree from Staley College, and the Star of Solidarity of the Italian Republic. His longstanding dream—to create an institution of higher learning—may come true in the establishment of the Dante University of America; and Forte will be recognized as one of its founders.

Perhaps we stand now on the frontier of a prejudice-free age. The son of simple parents, Felix Forte achieved fame and recognition; and in his success lies the hope that prejudice can indeed by conquered in the United States. A step toward this end will be taken when an Italian-American judge sits on the bench of the United States Supreme Court—not as a token instance of "equal opportunity," but as the natural consequence of that judge's intelligence, compassion, and sensitivity to the law. But ultimately, repjudice will be conquered not through appointments or elections, but through a growing recognition of the intrinsic value of each human being. And such a change of minds and hearts, unfortunately, is difficult to achieve.

144

GIOVANNI CASTANO (1896-1978): *Born in Calabria;* Died *in Massachusetts*

With the single exception of Luigi Palma di Cesnola (first director of the Metropolitan Museum of Art), Giovanni Castano has done more to enrich America's artistic heritage than any other Italian.

John—as his fellow artists and art experts call him—came to America from Gasperina in 1904. Gasperina, in the southern part of the colorful Calabrian region, is also the birthplace of Campanella, Mattia Preti (Il Calabrese), Cilea, and Boccioni. Though he left Italy when he was a child, Giovanni brought with him vivid impressions of the color, music, philosophy, and passionate humanity of the Calabrian people. Eighty-one years later, in his home in Needham, Massachusetts, he speaks of Calabria in the manner of a child nursing a fantastic but beautiful fairy tale.

Castano's paintings, recognizable by their elaborate floral colors, reflect his Calabrian background. A modern impressionist, he has also depicted scenes of America with as much love and passion as his native-born teachers and colleagues.

A graduate of the School of the Boston Museum of Fine Arts, Castano studied with Philip Hale, Leslie Thompson, Huger Elliot, F. M. Lamb, and Henry James. After graduation, he worked as a scenic artist in theatres and opera houses throughout the United States. He has painted murals for many churches and public buildings, and at the age of seventy-four, restored the Herter murals at the Boston State House. He has also restored hundreds of canvasses of various famous painters.

Castano has enriched the collections of the National Art Gallery, the Fogg Museum, the Boston Museum of Fine Arts, the Metropolitan Museum of Art, and the Toledo Museum. More important, when the preference of the American public turned to modern art, Castano worked in behalf of the great American traditionalists.

Castano has been the champion of these artists for many years. He preserved, appraised, and made known to the

145

Giovanni Castano.

Giovanni Castano, by Mortimer Lamb.

American public the works of such artists as Childe Hassam, Winslow Homer, Martin Johnson Meade, Fitz Hugh Lane, Washington Allston, Elihu Veder, William Morris Hunt, and Arthur Clifton Goodwin. (Another Italian, Lionello Venturi, worked to make these artists and their work known to the European public.) As a result of Castano's efforts, paintings that some forty years ago could not be sold for $100 are now being sold for $100,000.

We are all richer for Castano's inestimable contribution to our artistic heritage, but even more so for the example he set, offering the labor of his hands and the love in his soul.

GIOVANNI E. SCHIAVO (1898-   ): Born in Sicily; Living in Texas

Giovanni Ermenegildo Schiavo came to America at age eighteen, having completed high school in his native city of Trapani, Sicily. In America, he attended the Johns Hopkins, New York, and Columbia universities, which awarded him several generous scholarships. He has contributed to newspapers, magazines, and reference publications, including the *Encyclopedia Americana*. His forte, however, has been the history of the Italian-Americans. Were it not for his efforts, much of our knowledge of the contributions of these people would have been lost. In many ways, this book, itself, has been easier to write because of the basic, extensive research accomplished by Schiavo.

That his contribution has been vast can be seen from the following titles: *The Italians in Chicago; The Italians in America Before the Civil War; Italian-American History* (in two volumes); *What Crime Statistics Show About the Italians; Four Centuries of Italian-American History; Philip Mazzei, One of America's Founding Fathers; Antonio Meucci, Inventor of the Telephone; The Truth About the Mafia and Organized Crime in America; Italian-American Who's Who;* and *The Italians in Missouri.* He has also written a *Dictionary for Travelers,* as well as *The Scientific Achievements of Leonardo da Vinci.*

Schiavo's only limitation in completing the single, comprehensive history of America's largest ethnic group, is time, itself. So vast is the field, that many more Giovanni Schiavos are needed to do it justice. Yet with the exception of a few attempts by as few individuals, Schiavo has been alone. That he has done a yeoman's job is as much to his credit as it is of importance to America's historiography.

Historiography is the official history of a court or institution; and in the Italian culture, historiography enjoys a prominence equal to that of narrative prose. Italians have written several types of historiography—providential, humanistic, idealistic, and erudite—each presenting historical facts from a specific though ample viewpoint, with certain rules or guidelines applied throughout. As a historiographer, Schiavo is to Italian-American history what Herodotus was to the early Greek world, what Tacitus was to the world of the early Romans, what Villani and Compagni were to the world of the emerging Italian republics and city states. Schiavo might be considered the father of Italian-American history, having written the only comprehensive history of a people who can be proud of the heritage they will have left behind.

Neither the Italian-Americans nor the American citizens in general have paid Schiavo's work sufficient attention. Nevertheless, while he is working away in almost complete oblivion, such enterprises as the Arno Press are publishing many of his works. How ironic, incidentally, that the Arno Press, which Italian-Americans made into perhaps the world's largest publishing house, is now owned by the New York Times Corporation.

The editor of the Vigo Press (named after Francis Joseph Vigo, who explored the Northwest Territory), Mr. Schiavo may possibly achieve recognition only after his demise, when his books will at once become collector's items. Such is the fate of many great men and women.

Giovanni E. Schiavo.

ENRICO FERMI (1901-1954): *Born in Italy; Died in the United States*

Known in many circles as the father of the Atomic Age, Enrico Fermi was an Italian who bore witness to the discovery, control, and use of atomic power.

Fermi succeeded in achieving uranium fission at the University of Rome in 1930. Twelve years later in Chicago, he built the Fermi Pile, the first nuclear reactor, achieving the chain reaction that ushered in the Atomic Age. As a tribute to Fermi, the University of Chicago has dedicated a plaque which reads, "On December 2, 1942, man succeeded in producing a chain reaction for the first time, and so began the production of controlled nuclear energy."

Unfortunately for humankind, the Atomic Age brought with it the potential to destroy life to an extent unparalleled in human history. Luckily for us and the rest of the world, Enrico Fermi came to the United States—and not Germany or Russia—to reveal the secrets of the atom: had he done otherwise, he may well have contributed towards the victory of Nazism or Communism, and with it, the submission of the free world to a single power.

It is common knowledge that Germany, Russia, and Japan all attempted to build the superbomb that would have given them world dominance. What would have happened had the Italian scientist gone to them? We saw what happened in Japan with the two bombs; think what might happen with the M.I.R.V. systems already in the arsenals of the major powers!

Yet, like Einstein, who quickly understood the potentials of the atomic chain reaction, and made his understanding available to President Roosevelt, Enrico Fermi envisioned the peaceful usage of his discovery.

The Atomic Age was born out of necessity at a time of war; but the benefits it makes available to mankind are inestimable. In every field of endeavor, from recreation to the utilities to medicine, atomic power can be used to make unprecedented contributions. Let us hope and pray that the discoveries

Enrico Fermi: "Nobel Prize physicist, came to U.S. in 1939 as a pioneer in atomic energy. Author and teacher." (From the Victoria Mint.)

made by this great genius will be utilized to enhance the joys of life rather than for life's destruction.

LOUIS ROBERT PERINI (1903-1972): *Born and Died in Massachusetts*

The son of Bonfiglio and Clementina Perini, first-line immigrants from Brescia and Parma respectively, Louis Robert Perini became the owner and president of the Perini Corporation, one of the largest construction companies in the world.

Lou Perini, as he is generally known, was twenty-one years old when his father died in 1924. The young man inherited the reigns of a company which was already engaged in modest road and dam construction: enough work and the right amount of time for young Lou to learn about the construction business. Lou was also fortunate in having been exposed to his father's ways of doing things—to the Italian tradition of hard work, and to Bonfiglio's congeniality, basic native intelligence, and intuitiveness.

Under Lou's leadership, the Perini Corporation grew from a small regional company into an international organization that handled major contracts on practically every continet. From India to Africa to South America to Canada, his corporation has left lasting monuments.

In a way, this Italian-American has done nothing less than to continue the tradition of his Italian forefathers: Joseph Marini directed the South Indian Railways of Bombay and built the gigantic bridge on the Ganges. Luigi Negrelli may have had a larger role in building the Suez Canal than is otherwise known in the French- and English-speaking worlds. Andrea and Francis Matarazzo created Brasil's greatest industrial complex (for which Andrea was nominated Senator). And Moretti and Nervi built Canada's tallest skyscraper in Montreal.

Italians have also been responsible for such projects as the Upper and Kems Canal in France, the Trans-Siberian Railway, the Pekin-Hankow railway system in China, the Kariba Dam in Rhodesia, the Volta Dam in Ghana, the Awash Plant in Ethiopia, and the Watergate Complex in Washington, D.C. They also constructed the power and thermo-

155

Louis R. Perini (from *Perini Quarterly*).

electric plants in Brasil, Peru, Chile, Panama, South Korea, and Pakistan; the pipelines in Syria, Turkey, and Tanzania; and many other projects, including airports and shipyards throughout the world.

An impresario in the truest sense of the word, Perini supervised the following projects: Yuba River Development Project in Marysville; the California and the Golden Gateway centers in San Francisco; the Tahachapi Discharge Tunnels; the Amistad Dam; the Prudential Tower in Boston; the Massachusetts Turnpike Extension; the dams and locks for the St. Lawrence Seaway; and the world's largest long tunnels at Niagara Falls. The Perini company has also undertaken grandiose projects in South America, Australia, and the Middle East.

Lou was also involved with many civic and sports activities. During his tenure as president of the Braves National League Baseball Club, he was cited for "His courage and farsightedness" in paving the way for future baseball franchises.

Perini has left a legacy of consummate accomplishments that have brought credit to America's tradition of intelligent hard work and competitive spirit. The time may be ripe for a Perini—like Matarazzo in Brazil—to run for the Senate, or even the Presidency of the United States.

JOSEPH PELLEGRINO (1908—   ): *Born in Sicily; Living in Massachusetts*

"It's Prince Spaghetti Day!"—the slogan has been incorporated into the American language, just as pasta has become a staple of the American diet. Defying translation, the words "pizza" and "pasta"—like "hot dog" and "hamburger"— have become part of everyday language, not only in Italy and America, but also throughout Europe and in Japan.

Just about every modern nation has some spaghetti king. In England, Carlo Forte, who was recently knighted by the Queen, is known as "Mr. Piccadilly"; and it was he who showed the English that "spaghetti do not grow in the fields." If Sir Forte is among the most successful English-Italian entrepreneurs of all time, his American counterpart is Joseph Pellegrino, our own unknighted king of spaghetti.

Pellegrino, who came to America from Sicily when he was still a teenager, educated himself mainly at evening school. Even though his formal education was not outstanding, his intelligence and common sense enabled him to take control of a small, local, and faltering macaroni factory, and turn it into a giant company whose products compete successfully in many parts of the world.

As a teenager he sold shopping bags and shined shoes on the New York sidewalks, eventually earning enough money to buy a custard-making machine. When he earned enough from that enterprise, he was able to go into the wholesale grocery and shoe-repairing businesses.

At age twenty-three, he entered the macaroni business and soon had an interest in the Roma Macaroni Company in Long Island, which he quickly turned into a profit-making organization. Fate would have it that the company plant was destroyed by fire in 1940; and Pellegrino, forced to move to Boston, where he met with the Prince Macaroni executives. The following year, Pellegrino bought out the Prince Company, and moved the operation from Prince Street in Boston's North End to its present location in Lowell, Massachusetts.

It was as president of the Prince Spaghetti Company that

Joseph Pellegrino (from *The Boston Post*).

Pellegrino created the famous "non-skid" spaghetti—spaghetti that won't fall off your fork!—which was quickly acclaimed by spaghetti lovers throughout the land. He also began to experiment with the Italian *cucina* (the same cooking style that Catherine de Medici brought to France, where it became known as French cuisine) which he now serves at his Prince Grotto restaurant. *Pasta con broccoli, pasta al segreto, scua scua* sauce, *pollo alla marengo,* and *tagliatelle in casa* are but a few specialties of Pellegrino's Italian *cucina.*

Knighthood or not, Joseph Pellegrino has become the true Prince of Spaghetti. Thanks to his ingenuity, hard work, and tenacious efforts, pasta has become a "regular" on the American dinner table.

"It's Prince Spaghetti Day!"

You bet!

JOSEPH L. C. SANTORO (1908-): *Born in Cambridge; Living in Belmont, Massachusetts*

Joseph Santoro, who has received several awards, including two gold medals from the American Artist Professional League in New York, joins the ranks of America's outstanding artists. He has visited many countries and traveled extensively in the United States, depicting the countryside and the lifestyle in rich watercolors, with a sensibility reminiscent of the great masters of the past. Looking at his paintings, one is reminded of the great *acquarelles* of Giovanni Fattori, Italiam impressionist of the nineteenth century.

As an artist, Santoro shows deep feeling for his subjects, and he is remarkable for his use of color. His paintings, *Falmough Light, Winter at Good Harbor, Mexican Wash Woman*, and *Sicilian Woman* seem literally to be bathed in light. But perhaps the watercolors that best present this distinctive use of light are the gold-medal winners, *Fishing Boats, Saudi Arabia*, and *Reflections*.

Known as the "fighting artist," Santoro has been involved in both amateur and professional sports. As a young man, he fought in the ring to earn money for art lessons. He later became a boxing official, and has judged fights featuring Basilio, De Marco, Pep, Pender, Robinson, and many others.

Santoro is a member of the American Watercolor Society, the American Artist Professional League, the Allied Artists of America, the Rockport Art Association, and the Guild of Boston Artists. He is a self-made man and artist who has devoted his life to making America more beautiful.

His *Sicilian Woman* sits on a stone wall, the sun's rays lighting her face and falling on the houses in the background. Perhaps she is pondering the story of Sicily, itself—the hundreds of foreign invasions, the corruption imposed upon her people, the arid but beautiful landscape. Through the stormy history of her people, the Sicilian woman— Sontoro's essential Sicilian woman—endures. She has given birth to such individuals as Archimedes, Vincenzo

161

Sicilian Woman, by Joseph L.C. Santoro.

Bellini, Giovanni Verga, Luigi Pirandello, Salvatore Quasimodo, Elio Vittorini, and others.

She is perhaps pondering a greater human irony—the unwarranted injustices and prejudices perpetrated on her children.

VINCENT THOMAS LOMBARDI (1913-1970): *Born in Brooklyn; Died in Washington*

Rocky Marciano retired undefeated. Phil Esposito has broken all kinds of records in hockey. And Vincent Lombardi—Vince, as he was known in the sports world—was a legend in his own lifetime.

It is amazing just how many Italian names stand out in the history of sports: in *baseball*—Berra, Lazzeri, Crosetti, Cavaretta, Di Maggio, Garagiola. In *football*—Savoldi, Carideo, Iacavazzi, Bellino, Getto, Macaluso, Trippi, Guglielmi, Perilli, Robustelli, Piccolo, Marchetti, La Monica, Cappelletti, Pastorino, Canadeo, Lavelli, Nomellini.

In *bowling*—Romaniello, Fazio, Scalia, Donato, Salvino, Petraglia, Fargalli. In *golf*—Turnesa, Urzetta, Manera, Venturi, Caponi, Sarazen, Revolta, Ghezzi. In *billiards*—Ponzi, Mosconi. In *boxing*—Bettina, Pastrano, Graziano, La Motta, Giardello, De Marco, Basilio, Canzoneri, Battalino, Papaleo, Marino, D'Agata.

In *rifle and pistol*—Ciavarelli, Melagrano. In *horse racing*—Colangelo, Rubbicco, Venezia, Belmonte, Valenzuola, Arcaro. In *Auto racing*—Granatelli, DePalma, Andretti. And in *bocce*, Varipapa, Santore, Spinella, Fargalli, and Spartano.

As for Vincent Lombardi, what can be said about this football coach—a first-generation American of Italian descent —whose teams have won several National and two World Championships? Who has repeatedly led mediocre and even losing teams to one victory after another? Who has won the admiration and affection of such football greats as Jerry Kramer, Sonny Jurgenson, Jimmy Taylor, Bart Starr, and many, many others? Had not death called Lombardi at the height of his success, what else would he have done?

Vince has been elected to the Football Hall of Fame. The name Vincent, incidentally, derives from the Latin *vincens*— "winning," a participial form of *vincere*—"to win." How descriptive of a man who admonished his teams, "Winning

Vince Lombardi: "Hall of Famer, he led his teams to 3 national
& 2 world titles." (From the Victoria Mint.)

is not everything. It is the only thing!" He added, on one occassion, that what endures is "the will to excel and the will to win."

ROCKY MARCIANO (1923-1969): *Born in Brockton, Mass.;*
Died in the Midwest

A great moment in the history of boxing—the thirteenth-round knockout of world heavyweight champion Jersey Joe, on September 23, 1952—belongs to Rocco Marchegiano.

It happened in Philadelphia: "Rocky Marciano," twenty-nine years old and weighing in at 186 pounds, entered the ring as challenger to Joe Walcott, nine years older, and weighing in at 196 pounds. Jersey Joe, setting the pace at the start of the first round, floored the challenger, who was made to take the count before he could get on his feet. For the next thirteen rounds, Joe continued to dominate the fight, battering his opponent.

Then unexpectedly, bleeding from many cuts and wobbling from Walcott's furious blows, Marciano plunged with his left, and followed with a quick right. Another powerful right to the jaw sent Walcott to the canvas for good. The knockout gave Marciano the world heavyweight championship; and he was to retain the title until he retired in 1956. He held his title for a longer period than any other champion (Gene Tunney also retired undefeated, but after only two years of fighting).

Rocky, who received the Edward J. Neil Memorial Award in 1952, earned more money directly from the ring than any fighter in the history of boxing. But he should not be praised for his boxing skill alone: his quiet, sportsmanlike manner won him the admiration of friends and foes-in-the-ring alike. He is one of many Italians the world over who, overcoming many adversities, actualized in the most inimitable ways his will to win. In each case, one must wonder where all the energy comes from.

Rocky Marciano: "World Heavyweight Champion. Retired Undefeated. 49 pro fights. 43 K. C.'s, 6 decisions." (From the Victoria Mint.)

BIBLIOGRAPHY

Beccaria, Cesare. *Opera*. Firenze: Sansoni, 1968.

Caso, Adolph. *Alfieri's Ode to America's Independence*. Boston: Branden Press, 1976.

_____. *America's Italian Founding Fathers*. Boston: Branden Press, 1976.

Dictionary of American Biography. New York: Charles Scribner's Sons, 1934.

Dizionario Enciclopedico della Letteratura Italiana. Bari: Laterza, 1967

Imperatori, Ugo. *Dizionario di Italiani all'Estero*. Genova: L'Emigrante, 1965.

Iorizzo, L. and S. Mondello. *The Italian Americans*. Twayne, New York: Cecyle S. Neidle, 1971.

Marraro, H.R. *Filippo Mazzei*. New York: Columbia University Press, 1942.

Mazzei, Filippo. *Vita E Preregrinazioni del Fiorentino Filippo Mazzei*. Milano: Marzorati, 1970.

Musmanno, Michael. *The Italians in America*. New York: Doubleday, 1965.

National Cyclopedia of American Biography. New York: J. T. White, 1935.

New Catholic Encyclopedia. Washington, D.C., 1967.

Rossi, Nick and Sadie Rafferty. *Music Through the Centuries*. Boston: Bruce Humphries, 1967.

Salvadori, Massimo. *The Italian People*. New York: Crown Publishers, 1972.

Schiavo, Giovanni E. *Four Centuries of Italian American History*. New York: The Vigo Press, 1955.

_____. *Italian-American Who's Who*. New York: The Vigo Press, 1935.

Taylor and Giordani. *Who's Who in Italy*. Milano, Intercontinental Books, 1958.

Vittorini, Domenico. *Attraverso I Secoli*. New York: Holt, Rinehart and Winston, 1957.

The World of Music. New York: Abradale Press, 1963.

INDEX

174

175